GREATER
THAN THE GAME

STEVIE *Shakespeare* BAGGS JR.

GREATER
THAN THE GAME

STEVIE *Shakespeare* BAGGS JR.

*"Stevie Baggs is one of the only players
who never allowed what he couldn't
do interfere with what he could do"*

Alvin Wyatt
Former NFL & current NCAA
head football coach

LIFE SCIENCE PUBLISHING™
YESTERDAY'S WISDOM;
TODAY'S DISCOVERY

Life Science Publishers
1216 South 1580 West, Ste. A
Orem, UT 84058
www.lifesciencepublishers.com
ISBN: 978-0-9905100-2-4

Printed in the United States of America.

This publication is designed to provide entertainment value and is sold with the understanding that the publisher is not engaged in rendering legal, accounting, or other professional advice of any kind. If legal advice or other expert assistance is required, the services of a competent professional person should be sought.

—From a Declaration of Principles jointly adopted by a Committee of the
American Bar Association and a Committee of Publishers and Associations
Cover Design by Roberto of DigimoPrinting.com
Editing by Life Science Publishing

Author & Motivational Speaker

"Some may teach you how to be great at a game,
but this book will teach you how to be Greater Than The Game."
StevieBaggsJr.com

Book Stevie for your next event: bookings@steviebaggsjr.com
Use Twitter/Facebook/Instagram Icons: @steviebaggsjr #GreaterThanTheGame

A portion of sales goes to the CETAFoundation.org

CONTENTS

"What Stevie Baggs meant to me: On Saturday afternoons during the football season I would start breaking down game film of the next opponent. Devising a game plan was always so easy because our defense was lead by a great team captain. The game plan was simple, I would devise our 50 defense to stop only one half of the field so that 10 players could defend it easily. Stevie Baggs had to defend the other half. He was that type of player that when ever we defended the option offense, Stevie could play the fullback, quarterback, and pitch back all by himself with no help from anyone else. His ability to play was an asset to me as a Defensive Coordinator, but his ability to LEAD was even a greater asset to me because opposing teams feared him. Stevie Baggs made me look good!"

Coach Brian Shafer
Lake Brantley High School

ACKNOWLEDGMENTS

I'd like to start off by saying that I can't possibly thank everyone who individually impacted my life to help me become GREATER THAN THE GAME however those of you whom are not individually mentioned please charge it to my head and not my heart.... The most important thing in this world to me is my interpersonal relationship with the Most High God whom created this universe and without I would not be able to tap into the supernatural ability that was placed on me to live a life GREATER THAN THE GAME. I'd like to thank my family (grandparents, uncles, aunts, cousins, teammates, friends, etc.) especially my parents Stevie Baggs Sr/Perry Robinson Sr. and Lola Cannon-Robinson/Valerie Buford-Baggs as well as my younger brother Devin Baggs. I'd like to also thank my other younger brothers and sisters for your love and continued support Raje, Makiya, and Malik. To my Uncle Tyrone "Tank" Alston who has always shown me the example of what a real man should be, faithful to your purpose as well as your God and family, you are my hero. Not to mention all the folks that aren't my blood relatives but may as well be, Demaral Beasley thanks so much for your advice and wisdom over the years and for being the example of what a mentor should truly be. To my other mentors who have fed into my life, without you I wouldn't possibly be the man that I am today. To all my former coaches and trainers, this list goes on and on from my sportsman days up to this point now being an actor. I know that the many coaches and trainers in my life who believed in me, did so with the love that it takes to pull greatness out of a person and I'm truly thankful because that same passion now lives in me to help pull greatness out of others. To my spiritual leaders and advisors, your prayers and insight has given me the strength and faith to carry-on in the midst of adversity, as well as the humility to stay grounded even during the highest peeks in my life and the strength to keep pushing during those valley moments. I would like to pay homage to my Canadian family that has played the role of mom and dad during so many times in my life and has treated me like a son since day one. Cesar and Sina Sacco I love you and appreciate your love and support over these years. I will always be your son. The folks whom I have lost in the natural, yet that have taught me the meaning of purpose through their life journey you may be gone but not forgotten: To my dear grandmother Rosa Mae Cannon, I love you and I miss you. You showed me what the word class, mercy, and grace really means. You also lived a life for God like none other, your prayers still live within me. Grandfather James Cannon, you will be missed. I loved your infectious smile, it shines through me today. Godmother Mayor Yvonne Scarlett-Golden, you were always such an inspiration and your accomplishments only epitomize your passion for people and life that you lived. Also, thank you for encouraging me to come back to Bethune-Cookman University to finish my degree. Although school is not for everyone education is and I learned that principal from you. To Coach Richard Harris, thank you for believing in my ability when no one else at the pro level did. Your vision to help me show everyone else that I did in fact have what it takes to win at the highest level will never be forgotten. I will never forget the days after practice when we sat down and talked about all of the many life lessons that the game of football has taught us. Thank you coach Harris. To Professor Dr. William Ziegler, I highly appreciate being under your tutelage as a student at Bethune-Cookman University. You helped me broaden my vision to see past the U.S. soil and to major in International Business. Thank you for always encouraging me even when I didn't realize my own intellectual ability. You helped me hone in on what it truly means to become an upstanding business man. To Aunt Francis Cannon, you defied the odds your whole life and its only right that you are now being honored this way. You always taught me to be strong but it wasn't until I saw you at your weakest point battling the terrible disease, pancreatic cancer, that I understood the true importance of taking care of my temple/body and living a balanced lifestyle and how true strength is measured by ones spirit not by ones might. To my educational institutions over the years I thank you. Highlands Christian Academy (elementary), Pompano Beach middle school, Lake Brantley High school and Bethune-Cookman University. If it were not for all of the people, places, and things mentioned above, along with those whom I did not mention, this book would not have been possible. To my unborn children, I want you to know that your Father loves you and that this will forever be a part of our family's legacy. God bless!!!

— Stevie "Shakespeare" Baggs, Jr.

My continuing journey in Faith led me directly to this incredible story and I genuinely hope that everyone who reads Greater Than The Game is better for it. For me, writing this book has absolutely changed my life. It sounds a little bit cliché maybe, but traveling down this path has opened my eyes to a whole new world. The writing experience allowed me to feel, understand, and address situations in my life that were holding me back. To me, Greater Than The Game is far more than just words printed on paper. I believe wholeheartedly in each one of the words, and I am living my best life guided by this extraordinary story.

While "thank you" seems wholly insufficient, it is my sincere hope Dad, Mom and Jaymes, that you will see my eternal gratitude flowing throughout the following pages. I love you all so very much. Stevie, I am humbled and grateful that you trusted me to share your amazing journey with the world. You have truly given me the courage to live my Greater Than The Game calling and I can never thank you enough for that. Stephen Copeland, I am beyond appreciative of your valuable work and willingness to share. The final product is a direct reflection of your hard work and dedication to this movement – "I wish there were more people in the world like you". Asha, Whitney and Aisha, you push, encourage, support and love me every day. Thank you, thank you, thank you. Finally, to my angel in heaven, I miss you so much. This book is a testament to how you continue to quietly move me to live far outside of my comfort zone.

I consider my greatest blessing in life to be the privilege of loving the amazing people who surround me. I am astounded by the outpouring of support from so many of you, especially those who have crossed my path in the most unlikely way. God is always right on time. My deepest gratitude to each of you who has encouraged and inspired me to live my dream without the expectation of anything in return.

— Krystyn Ordyniec

INTRODUCTION

Thank you. Yes you, reading this right now. Thank you for allowing me the absolute privilege to share my story and testimony through the pages of this book. Greater Than The Game is certainly not an epic novel so I expect that it will be a quick but valuable read. I know that your time is at a premium and I am grateful that you chose to invest it in my story. It is also worth noting that I want this journey together to be about practical self-discovery and transformation without getting caught up in complicated philosophical concepts. I assure you that you won't be disappointed and at the very least, it is my sincere hope that Greater Than The Game inspires you in some tangible way that you can share with the world. Now then, on with the show…

Greater Than The Game actually started out as an autobiography: "The amazing story of the amazing life of Stevie Baggs Jr."… Until that is, I realized the following very humbling fact: going through life and having some lousy things happen to me doesn't make me amazing or special. It makes me regular. And normal. And nobody wants to read a book about regular and normal. Let's face it, every person has a story to tell. Every person has been to Hell and back. And then on top of that, we all live to tell about it! So, luckily for the few of you whom I would have forced to read the book, I shelved the autobiography and thought long and hard about how I could actually use my story in a constructive fashion. I thought, if I can inspire just one person, to make one change, or to look at their situation just a little bit differently, my story will be worth sharing. I know that doesn't really make me special either, but writing about my life experiences thus far does afford me the incredible opportunity to connect with people through the power of words and to reach people that I might never have otherwise been able to meet personally.

As you are going through the chapters of this book, I urge you to take my stories and substitute your own. Your name instead of mine. Your circumstances and life experiences instead of mine. By doing so, you will get so much more out of Greater Than The Game and you will help me to accomplish my goal of spreading the important messages instead of getting caught up in the details of my life. I use the stories only so that you can appreciate where I am coming from and I can tell you this right now, I am by no means an expert on life and I am far from perfect (as you will soon see). If you can close your eyes and think of a time in your life that in some way parallels my particular anecdotes, you will get exactly what I want you to get out of the experience. And by experience, I mean it. I want you to go to the social media pages to share your stories, pictures, thoughts and feelings. I want you to listen to the video blogs and interact with me. I don't want Greater Than The Game to start and end with words that you see written here, I want it to be a movement and the only way that I can accomplish that goal is for you to participate in the movement. I don't care if you can't remember one thing that happened in Stevie Baggs Jr.'s life when you put this book down. If however, you can use my stories to examine, evaluate, enrich and enlighten your life and the lives of the people around you, I will consider the book a huge success.

As for me, I really am just a regular guy. A guy who has played on 11 professional Football teams, in 10 seasons, in the National Football League (NFL), NFL Europe, the Arena Football League and the Canadian Football League (CFL). Sound surreal? Sometimes I feel like it is, but I can now appreciate that is my personal Football story, and one that I certainly think makes my career unique if nothing else. If you personally enjoy the sport of Football, you will definitely like some of the references that I use, but I promise you that I will not bore you with the details of the game if Football isn't really your thing.

I was born in Fort Lauderdale, Florida and spent the majority of my formative years in Pompano Beach, Florida. I am a South Florida native and although I currently reside in Atlanta, Georgia, I still consider Florida home. Growing up, my Family had its share of ups and downs; some very typical of a normal Family, and some a little bit more personal to my life. Throughout those years, there were very few constants in my life, but I consider my Faith, Family relationships and Football to be those things that helped me through it all. My parents divorced just before I went to high school, and I found myself enrolled at Lake Brantley High School in Alamante Springs, Florida. Given the upheaval in my Family life, I seriously considered not playing Football at all that year; however, for whatever reason, I suited up my first year and I am pretty glad that I did because I went on to set the State of Florida all time single-season high school sack record in my senior year at Lake Brantley. Later on, I was a three-time All-American at Bethune-Cookman University, also in Florida. Despite all of the accolades, promises and dreams, however, I found myself undrafted in the 2004 NFL Draft. This is when the toughest years of my Football life began, and I bounced around from the AFL, to NFL Europe, to the CFL, to the NFL, and back through each of the leagues once again. Sometimes maybe twice. Throw in some odd jobs as a truck driver, a substitute teacher, a waiter, a personal trainer and an actor, and this winding journey is precisely why I am where I am today, delivering to you Greater Than The Game. The years of rejection, triumph, tragedy, comedy, lessons, valleys and peaks, this is why I am able to share my story with you. You see, in school you are taught a lesson, and then you are tested on that lesson. Life happens just the opposite: you are tested, and then it is up to you to figure out what that lesson is. This book is a culmination of all of the lessons that I have discovered along my journey. Think of it almost like a little hint sheet that you wish that you could have brought into the final exam. I can't tell you the answers, but I hope that I can help you to reach your own truth. It could have all started and ended with Football. Instead, I believe that Football has equipped me in my journey to become Greater Than The Game and is what has ultimately allowed me to fulfill my life's purpose away from the field.

I am here to remind you throughout this journey together that we are all Greater Than The Game. Often times, the clearest example of the game manifests itself in the form of a job or career. Whether that vocation is a stay-at-home parent, business executive, administrative assistant, doctor, attorney, teacher, barista, entertainer, athlete, nurse, engineer, waitress, caregiver or dog-walker, the principles remain the same. The game extends far beyond your career however, and includes any or all of the circumstances, situations and conditions that personally affect you. The key to living a purposeful life is addressing the aspects of your game that could benefit from some improvement. As a Football player, you work every day at becoming faster, stronger, more agile, more educated about the game. All facets of Football require total dedication to the game both on and off the field and similarly, you must demand that same degree of commitment from yourself so that you can live your best life.

Do your relationships need improvement? Perhaps you have unfulfilled goals that just keep getting shelved. Maybe you live with constant feelings of resentment towards certain people in your life, or debilitating anxiety about money. Or you look in the mirror everyday and don't really like the person you see staring back at you. Whatever aspect of your game that needs changing, you are the only person in the world who has the complete power to actually make those changes. Think about that for a minute. Isn't that amazing? You hold the power and I am here to help you unleash that power. If making meaningful change was really that easy, we would all be living perfect lives, and as humans I am sure that we can all agree that perfection doesn't exist. We are constantly in transition and transformation and it is recognizing the value that the difficulties and struggles within that change hold as related to our personal growth. The valley moments prepare you for your mountaintop moments. You don't get to the peak of the mountain by starting anywhere but from the bottom. At the same time, remaining stagnant in the important areas of your life, even if everything seems to be moving along ok, doesn't help you to mature and evolve. It actually holds you back. Do you just want to be hanging out in the middle of the mountain forever? Life operates in a state of flux and if we can embrace both the positives and negatives of the journey with assistance of the powerful tools that we hold within us, we can and will be unstoppable.

I have concentrated this book on 7 concepts, or tools to the game as I like to call them, that I will share with you throughout our journey in the following chapters: 1) Faith; 2) Family; 3) Focus; 4) Finances; 5) Fitness; 6) Forgiveness and 7) Football. Maybe just one will resonate with you. That's ok. Maybe all 7 will hit home. That's ok too! Collectively, these 7 "F's" have shaped my individual insight and understanding that I am far greater than each and every one of the many rejections and disappointments that I have experienced both on the Football field, and in life. I can unequivocally say the same for you, and I probably haven't even met you. How can I do that you might ask? Because I know that we are all inherently Greater Than The Game. We are all called to a greater purpose here in our limited time on earth. Some of us just have to work a little bit harder to tap into and harness the infinite resources waiting to be released. This is not an easy road, but as with most journeys worth taking, the first step is always the most difficult and I thank you again for taking that initial leap with me.

To help my points resonate with you more deeply, you will notice that each one of the "F's" has been purposely capitalized whenever it is used throughout the book. It is my hope that by doing this, your awareness will be further heightened as to the importance of the concept. Through careful personal reflection of the 7 "F's", I believe that you too will be able to identify, cultivate, and share the gifts that make you so special. Others may teach you how to become great at a game. My genuine hope is that this book will assist your personal journey to becoming Greater Than The Game.

"Stevie Baggs is the most enthusiastic motivated player that I have ever been around... Stevie got our team and defense ready to believe in themselves as they never believed in anything else before in their life... Stevie is the only player that I knew would never ever ever at any time let what he couldn't do interfere with what he can do... With that mindset at such a young age, I believe that is what propelled him to be one of the most outstanding student athletes in Bethune-Cookman University history."

Alvin Wyatt
Former NFL player & head coach for
Bethune-Cookman University

CHAPTER 1

FAITH

"Foundation Abiding in Truth High-Up".

Close your eyes and imagine for a minute that you are in the process of planning and building your dream home. You meet with an architect to draw the plans, with contractors to pick out the finishes, and an interior design team to put your personal touch on the design of the home. The home is built and you throw a housewarming party so that everyone can come and tell you how beautifully everything turned out. Now imagine that you failed to adequately address the necessity of the foundation of the home, using inexpensive materials that could not withstand the weight of the structure. What happens? Your dream home quickly begins to crack and it will eventually fail completely. One bad storm and the entire home is gone. You don't see the foundation when you look at all of the esthetically pleasing aspects of the home, but you know that it's there and that it's one of the most important parts of the viability of the home. Now think for a moment about your life. What sort of foundation are you building your every day experiences on? Is your foundation strong like concrete? Is it rooted in a spiritual power that has been successfully relied upon for centuries and can withstand the storms that are certain to pass through? Or is it more like sand. Rooted in the secular nature of the pleasures here on earth and sure to collapse at the first sign of trouble. Think about it. We all have a foundation that guides our daily steps even if we are not consciously aware, and without that foundation, we would crumble like the proverbial home. The question then becomes is that foundation grounded in Faith, or personal gratification. Consider that every day we are faced with decisions that must be made, each directed by that personal foundation.

Some of those decisions are trivial and we may not be aware that we are actually making a choice; but in turn, some decisions have much more at stake. I can honestly say the most important decision I ever made in my life came when I was faced with the choice to remain Faithful in God's ultimate plan for my life, or to abandon Him for my selfish view that he had essentially left me high and dry. I was at a crossroads, and the decision on which I chose to build my foundation was really one of life and death.

My introduction to the concept of Faith was quite humble and came through my upbringing in an all-black Pentecostal Christian community at Firstborn Church of the Living God in Pompano Beach, Florida. Women couldn't even wear pants! Knowing what I know now, it was a somewhat of a closed-minded community, but at the time my Family felt very comfortable there. My father was ordained a Deacon and my mother was a missionary through the church. Over time and through my experiences in college and Football, I gradually began to have a more inclusive view of Faith than what I was initially exposed to, and quickly figured out that 'my way' of practicing Faith was certainly not the only one. I am now comfortable in saying that having Faith and belonging to a church transcends the boundaries of the four walls which enclose the church's structure, and true ministry occurs every day outside of those four walls.

It was not until the summer of 2007, however, that it became clear to me that the traditional concepts of Faith and religion that we come across every day are really just a series of relationships. Relationships with each other, relationships with a higher being, and a relationship with yourself. Relationships are what have ultimately taught me the tough life lesson that: "I am not the center of the universe, and the sun and moon do not revolve around my personal experiences". And trust me, there have been more than a few times in my life that I really believed that it all started and ended with me.

I travelled to Winnipeg, Manitoba in May, 2007 optimistic about the upcoming Football season with the CFL's Winnipeg Blue Bombers. After a season with Winnipeg in 2006 that I have tried (somewhat unsuccessfully) to completely forget about, the coaching staff assured me that I would have a prominent role in the team's defensive scheme; however, I soon came to the realization after being put on the team's practice roster for a second season, that was not the way it was going to all play out. I left Winnipeg and signed with the CFL's Edmonton Eskimos, only to be disappointed once again. Back in, you guessed it, Winnipeg, I found myself earning $400 (Canadian dollars, let's be clear) per week. I was living out of the back of my car, and at the same time, constantly worrying about how I was going to make payments on that car which doubled as my bed at night. Not to mention, I had a condo in Florida that wasn't exactly paying for itself. I could barely afford to eat, let alone even begin to come to terms with the fact that I was actually homeless. All I could Focus on was the age old selfish question: Why in the world is this happening to me?

I don't know exactly what brought me to ring the doorbell at Cesare Sacco's home that day, but I can certainly tell you that I swallowed every single ounce of pride I had before doing so, and I actually think that I was completely numb to my dire situation. I guess looking back now I didn't really have any other option. Cesare was a CFL official at the time I was playing in Winnipeg and we had socialized on a few occasions so he wasn't a complete stranger. After graciously allowing me to take a much-needed nap (trust me, I looked like death warmed over and still I have no idea why they even let me in the front door, but I digress…), I explained to Cesare and his wife, Sina, that if I did not find a place to stay soon, I would be forced to leave Winnipeg and move back south. To make a long story short, miraculously, after what I am sure was a very interesting and intense discussion, the Saccos invited me to live in their home. Absolute strangers had opened their home to me without question and without limitation. It wasn't too long before I felt like a real member of their Family. The Sacco's daughters, Jennifer and Ashleigh, routinely came to me for relationship, friendship and life advice, and instead of "Mr. and Mrs. Sacco" I soon began calling Cesare and Sina "mom and dad".

Let me paint this picture a little bit more clearly for you: the Saccos are a white, middle-class, Catholic Family who took in a black, homeless Football player that they knew absolutely nothing about, and shared their home, their food, and their hearts. Imagine opening your home to someone you don't know, how scary that must have been for them. But not once did the Sacco's ever make me feel as if I did not belong. I learned many Catholic traditions that were an important part of the Sacco's way of practicing Faith and this way of practice was a far cry from the strict Pentecostal upbringing I was accustomed to. What struck me most profoundly, however, was the daily realization that no matter what the religion of the people sitting around the table, above all we are connected by relationships with those people. Those same personal relationships are in turn the tie that binds us with whatever higher power we choose to identify with. It's not about titles, but about connections. Pentecostal or Catholic. Black or White. Canadian or American. It didn't matter. We were a Family brought together by something way beyond the denomination of the Faith that we practiced and the upbringing we experienced. The food served everyday at our table, was love. More recently, I have tried substituting the word relationship for the word religion in my vocabulary. Similarly, when I interact with people I consider the same concept because I find that practicing relationships instead of religion allows me to grow my Faith through those connections without the need for labels, titles and unnecessary conditions. Above all, we are all just people put on this earth to live out a plan that is much bigger than we are, and respecting that simple truth has helped me to grow my Faith in leaps and bounds.

Twenty-five years before I rang the Sacco's doorbell, Sina gave birth to a stillborn son, buried immediately after he was born. Had he still been alive today, we would have been just months apart in age. When talking about why I ended up at their house out of all the homes in Winnipeg, Sina once said to me with tears in her eyes, "I can't even begin to describe it. It was almost like God was saying 'I can't bring him back to you, but this is My way of giving you a son in your life". When it looked like I was going to be forced out of Winnipeg due to my poor financial situation, I was given a Family. In turn, I seemingly filled a void the Saccos had felt in their lives for so many years left by the death of their son. A series of relationships that taught me unconditional love, understanding, sacrifice, and Faith. Relationships that actually made me feel and bear witness to God's presence in my life. It was at the moment that I rang the Sacco's doorbell that I really and truly began to buy into that life and death decision that I mentioned earlier, the decision to choose Faith in God over trying to figure out 'why this was happening to me'. This is truly where the first and most important layers of my Faith-based foundation were laid.

God's awesome ways are alive and well in my life on a daily basis, but I use this poignant story to illustrate Faith as the understanding and commitment to believing in something greater than you at work in your life, no matter how you personally identify that concept. Too often we view situations and events in our lives under a tiny microscope, feeling as though things happen because of us. Trust me, you and I aren't that special. I assure you that most things in life happen in spite of what we do, how we think, what we feel, and how we act. Take yourself out of the equation, and more often than not the answer or outcome to a particular situation will be exactly the same. Why is that? Because there is always a power greater than you at work in your life. Something that you can't necessarily see, but that you can always feel. Tapping into the unknown is perhaps the most difficult commitment for some people to make because as humans, we are inherently scared to put trust in anything that we cannot visualize. Imagine though, that there is a power waiting to take on your burdens and worries and tough decisions. A power that doesn't ask anything in return, only that we unwaveringly believe and trust in its healing and loving ways. What the power is called remains up to you. I am definitely not here to preach to you about religious views, but take some time to really find out what it is that you connect with. Label it God, Allah, Jehovah, Lord, Maker, Creator, Master, Spirit, Universe; whatever it is, that powerful force transcends our human understanding. Faith is what allows us to unconditionally believe in that higher power no matter how bleak a passing moment may feel. Given that the mystery of Faith is difficult to tangibly explain, I believe that by cultivating relationships and respecting people with differing views we are able to actually experience the wondrous power of Faith through the normal course of our daily lives and we can strengthen our foundation through these important relationships.

I consider myself very blessed to have called numerous professional Football locker rooms my office for over a decade. Some of my teammates may just think it's crazy and might have packed in the Football dream a long time ago, but that's their prerogative. I got used to the questions, the looks, the comments, the judgment, the pretending to be happy for me when I moved into yet a new locker, on yet another team, in yet another country. Through my growing Faith,

I was confident that each move was just part of my journey, even when the rest of the world thought I was crazy. Being a social guy, it never took me very long to feel comfortable in a new environment, and one of the best perks of the job was getting to know my new teammates. I promise you that a professional Football locker room is filled with people of different personalities, different walks of life, and of course, differing Faiths.

I was also very quick to take a lead spiritual role amongst my new teammates. I was always leading the pre or post-game prayer, I made sure to attend chapel and bible study and encouraged others to do the same at every opportunity. I can tell you though, this role came with a lot of negative press. Being vocal about spirituality and my Faith put me in a prime position for ridicule and judgment every single day. That's not saying that my teammates were necessarily trying to be cruel about it because I think it was more that they were ignorant as to what I was actually trying to accomplish by keeping my Faith at the forefront of my life. That my Faith wasn't about them, but about me and my relationship with God and the foundation I wanted to keep building. It was probably much easier for my teammates to make a joke about me than to try and truly understand their own personal journeys with Faith. That, however, doesn't take away from the fact that their comments still hurt me. Perhaps most difficult for me to withstand was my teammates' constant judgment of my personal and relationship choices. It is helpful to remember that when faced with similar assassinations on your character by third parties, those opinions are absolutely none of your business. It is not about how they perceive you, but how you view yourself, and ultimately how your God views you. I will be the first to tell you that I very often fall short of the high expectations that I have for myself and certainly fall short of how I know that God wants me to live. That said, I know that I serve a God of Forgiveness and no matter how many times I fall, or disappoint Him, I will always be given another chance to be better. That is the power of Faith, knowing that no matter what happens, God still has my back. I know that when I speak to God about whatever it is that is troubling me, my Faith in Him will guide my decision. I have always lived by the saying, "I am not flawless, but I am Faithful". I know that when I put all of my trust in God and have Faith in His plans, I absolutely can't do anything to alter those plans, even if I make mistakes along the way. Hey, we are human and God knows that we are not perfect. That is what makes us so special.

Speaking of imperfect, for a long time, I operated as a "game day Christian". In other words, I served God specifically when it suited me best. One of my former teammates who practices a different religion from me posed the question, "why do so many Christians only claim God on game day?" He noticed that many of our peers gave glory to God only when they were in the spotlight. Whether it was through their pre-game rituals, touchdown dances, or post-game interviews, they were saying all the right things, at all the right times. He contemplated that these same players then lived the remainder of the week selfishly satisfying themselves, pursuing everything but God's path. For awhile, I was really no different. I claimed God's favor on game day, feverishly praying (and sometimes begging) that he would bless me on the field. I might have given Him some praise after a win, but during the week, after the game, it was all about me. I know that my foundation was weakest at these moments, ready to collapse at the slightest provocation. Over time and through crucial mentorship I gradually began to genuinely believe in the intimate and incredible relationship that God wants me to have with Him. I genuinely believed that my foundation has to be rooted in love and Faith and understanding and Forgiveness. Today I am confident that God's love for me is not a relationship that I can take for granted and call upon only in times of need. It is the single most important relationship that I have available to me and I must cherish and celebrate it to the fullest every day.

If we look at every event and feeling in our lives as a negative experience, it is extremely easy to feel as if we have been forsaken by God (or again, whatever higher power we choose to identify with). This is exactly what keeps many of us living in fear every day. Fear that we will not have enough money to cover this month's bills. Fear that we will be alone. Fear that our friends and Families do not understand or agree with what we are doing. When I said earlier that my decision to choose Faith was one of life or death, I really don't think that I was being overly dramatic. I could not possibly live the amazing life that I know is ahead of me if I chose fear instead of Faith because they are at totally opposite ends of the spectrum. Similarly, I could not look at my past as a wholly positive experience if the lens that I view it through is fear. I am so thankful for each of the trials, tribulations, relationships, jobs and experiences in my life. They are what made me the man I am today and the man that I strive to become in the future. If I chose fear instead of Faith, I would essentially have been spiritually dead, and to me, that's just not life worth living. We must make a concerted effort to choose Faith over fear in absolutely everything that we do, and I will also be the first to tell you that it is not easy. But you know what, it's possible. The most wonderful thing about our journey is that we have the power to consciously choose. So I challenge you to make the right choice, to slowly and deliberately assess and build up your personal foundation with the strong materials of Faith every single time that you are faced with a significant decision. Sometimes we don't know why we are tested by certain trials over the course of our lives. Just remember this: God gives his hardest tests to his strongest soldiers. That's all you have to know, that you are protected and loved through the power of your Faith and your foundation will never falter as long as it is built on those promises of protection. God never gives us more than we can handle. You will be amazed at how quickly you will begin to take the first steps in becoming Greater Than The Game simply by switching up your thought process and allowing your foundation to be rooted in the incredible strength of your Faith.

CHAPTER 2

FAMILY

"Flesh and blood, rich or poor, good or bad; through all these things, the only constant that I can count on is Family"

One thing that we can all probably agree on is that we have a Family. But that is likely where the agreement will end, and very quickly. To some, the concept of Family brings fond memories of a white picket fence, lemonade on the porch, children laughing, baking cookies, all coupled with feelings of inclusiveness, love, and support. To others, Family is just the opposite with thoughts of endless arguments, insufferable Family functions, the longing for a relationship with a disowned Family member, disputes brought on by substance abuse, and general feelings of hatred, loneliness and disappointment. And then there is all of the stuff in between those two extremes, which I am confident that the majority of us can relate to: the aunt that just won't stop asking when you're going to get married, the cousin that you just want to roll your eyes at for yet another stupid decision, elderly grandparents who make the already long Sunday dinner that much more of a production. The fact is, no matter how much they get on our nerves, they are still our Family. And I can almost guarantee that one day we will all look back on certain situations and wish that we had just a little more patience, said "I love you" just one more time, or gave someone just one last hug.

Look at the majority of people and more often than not their Family relationships directly reflect their outlook on life, decision-making processes, and relationships with others. That said, it is entirely feasible that we could blame our Family for absolutely everything that goes wrong in our lives. How many times have you heard the saying, "she came from the wrong side of the tracks, so we knew she would end up like that". Isn't that easy? Blame it on someone else. Well I don't buy that. I believe that we all have the ability to make positive and empowering decisions so that we will not just fall victim to circumstance. I believe that we all have the power to use our individual stories of the past to better our present situation and to completely change both our future and our Family's future.

My mother met my father when she was in high school, and much to my grandfather's annoyance, they began to date exclusively. Not long after, my mother was pregnant with me. And she was scared. Terrified in fact. She feared raising a child in the same poverty-stricken situation she grew up in, and still lived in. It was her worst nightmare as she puts it, to bring an innocent child into exactly the same circumstances that she herself was desperately trying to get out of. Add to that the almost-daily pressure to have an abortion exerted on her by her own father. You see, my grandfather probably didn't care all that much that my mother was pregnant, just that she had chosen the "wrong man, from the wrong Family, from the wrong side of town" to have a baby with. He was more interested in my mother associating with the "haves" and it killed him that she loved a "have not" as he so eloquently put it. I know that my mother was devastated by my grandfather's reaction and his remarks like "the bigger you get, the more disgusted I'm going to be" cut to her inner core. Imagine your father looking at you with such hate and disdain, it's a wonder that my mother was able to cope at all.

You can probably guess that my mother and father did not succumb to the pressure of their respective Family and friends, and by the grace of God, I was born just after my mother finished her senior year of high school. My parents were young and inexperienced. They didn't have a penny to their names and certainly didn't have the necessary Family support to be able to rely on any sort of regular help. On top of that, they lived for partying, even after I was born. Nothing really mattered to them at the beginning of my life more than having a good time. I would be willing to bet that at this time, the foundation on which my parents operated was extremely weak, rooted in pleasure and fun. But that soon changed. My parents took responsibility for me. They made decisions based on my well-being instead of their own. They surrounded me with friends and always put me first, even if it made their lives that much more difficult. When I look back at my humble beginnings, it would have been so easy for my parents to use the excuses that they were young, broke, barely educated, and came from nothing to justify that they couldn't raise me in a stable, loving and supportive environment. Instead, my mother and father collectively chose those circumstances as motivation so that the cycles of poverty, neglect and helplessness would not be perpetuated. My parents married not too long after I was born, and I have very fond memories of my childhood. Of course we struggled along the way, but my parents never allowed those struggles to come before my happiness. They were selfless when it came to raising me, determined not to allow their unpleasant Family situation and upbringing to hinder my growth. Early on, my father was also faced with serious pressure from his mentor to accept one of the Football scholarships offered to him by the Universities of South Carolina and West Virginia. He did not take either. Instead of listening to others, my parents listened to their hearts and chose me. But it might not have ended so well for me had my formative years been filled with feelings of guilt and blame because of that choice to raise me. I can honestly tell you though, not once did I ever feel like I was a mistake. Not once did my parents resent me for getting in the way of 'other' things in life. My parents made a decision, stuck with that decision, and never looked to blame anyone else for that decision. In turn, that decision was a turning point for my Family in a very positive way given that the odds were initially stacked against us.

You see, too often we feel immense pressure from our Family to go to certain schools, marry certain people, pursue certain careers, attain certain goals, make certain decisions, and sometimes those schools, people, careers, goals and decisions don't match what we see for ourselves in our future. And therein lies the key. The future is yours. Your future belongs to no one except you because you are the only one who has to live it. I am willing to bet that the majority of time our Family members really do have our best interests at heart, but at the same time, they are always viewing our lives through their personal lenses. Maybe your father wanted you to go medical school because his Family just didn't have the money to send him and it was always his dream to be a doctor. Maybe your Family says you can't possibly go to medical school because no one else in the Family ever went to school, let alone graduated and became a doctor. The choice really is, let someone else make decisions for us because of the past, or make decisions for ourselves in the present, for our future.

As we talked about in the previous chapter, we all have the power to choose and those choices dictate the paths that guide our life's journey. I am a firm believer that if we allow others to make a decision for us, positive or negative, we will forever hold some type of resentment towards the third party for that decision. On the other hand, if we make a decision that is from the heart, we take greater responsibility for that decision. Forever hold resentment towards Family? Or take personal responsibility. To me, the choice is always crystal clear. The problem is, sometimes Family will make it seem as if their way is the only way, or certainly the best way to do something. It is very likely that the truth will be somewhat disguised in this situation, and my best advice to you is to always follow your heart no matter what. If you make a mistake, it will be a learning experience for you and you have absolutely no one else to blame. If you only listen to Family however, your relationship may be forever tainted, and you may always resent them for the hurt that the decision might have caused. That said, it is important to always be aware of why you are making decisions, and not let past Family situations influence your present outlook for those decisions. Not allowing your Family to define your future, but at the same time respecting the past, is one of the earliest lessons I learned in becoming Greater Than The Game. Had it happened a little differently for me, I wouldn't even be in the game today.

After the disaster that was my NFL Draft Day (more about that to come), I tried my hardest to Focus on anything and everything completely unrelated to Football. Because of the rigorous demands of my Football and training schedule, I was one semester shy of obtaining my degree in Business Administration at Bethune-Cookman. I always intended to go back to finish my degree, but of course I figured it would be after a long career in the NFL and certainly didn't ever think that it would have been the fall I 'should' have been playing in my first NFL game. Well, there I was, back at Bethune-Cookman and let me tell you, that was a huge blow to my ego. I still consider it one of the most humbling experiences that I have been through. I would run into people on campus, and they would innocently ask, "What are you doing here?", "Why are you back?", or "What happened to playing Football?" They just didn't know any better. They had no idea that I had spent my summer in Football hell. But it was humbling, nonetheless, to be continually reminded that I didn't quite make it as a professional Football player- yet. Most people just asked me because they were curious. The majority of people, once I told them I was still pursuing my Football career but wanted to finish my degree, were supportive. Some though, I know were happy to see me fail. I completed the fall term with a sense of pride and accomplishment, and all of a sudden I found myself walking across the graduation stage, the first person from my entire extended Family to graduate from college. The experience was so much more rewarding than I ever thought possible. I went to school, honestly, just to play Football. At the beginning, graduating was secondary to the Football dream. But on my graduation day, my mother said to me, "Stevie, you don't have to pursue Football for us to be proud of you. We support you in your dream, but we are really proud of you because of this". Wow. All of a sudden I felt a new sense of responsibility to instill an education-based mindset in my younger Family members and to challenge them to also attend college. I continue to preach to anyone who will listen, the benefits of a college degree that go far beyond the degree itself. I went to school because of Football, and I graduated in spite of Football, and that forever changed my life and the future of my Family. I will always remember the feeling when my younger brother Devin and I had a moment alone during my graduation party and he looked at me and said, "I'm so proud of you". His words came from a place of genuine respect and love for what I had accomplished. I thought Football was the only way that my Family could be proud of me, and that was so far from the truth. I have always said that I believe that education is for everyone, but school may not be. I am so grateful that at this time in my life it was my season to finish that degree and use it to inspire and hold my Family accountable to work harder and accomplish things they may have not thought were possible.

Graduating from college is certainly not the only way you can change the course of your Family's future. There are so many positive steps that we can take to transform our situation and the key is not letting the past keep you from doing something differently. No one in your Family did it? Do it anyway! Every person in your Family did it? Don't do it! Refuse to be a product of your environment if there is something that you don't like. Easier said than done? Maybe not. Small steps lead to big results as long as you can keep an open mind and have a positive attitude. Do not to let the past be your excuse. I think you will be surprised at how much of an impact you can have in changing the game for not only yourself, but also your Family when you refuse to let your history define you.

During my fifth year at Bethune-Cookman, I worked as an assistant campaign manager for my godmother, Yvonne Scarlett-Golden, who was running for re-election as the mayor of Daytona Beach. I can't even begin to explain how much she taught me. She had an infectious love for people, and even though she had every opportunity to make a lot of money, she instead used her powerful position as a blessing to others through her years of service in public office. She just had an incredible impact on every single person she came into contact with. Yvonne also had a very influential effect on the city of Daytona itself given that she was Daytona's first African-American mayor and the first woman ever elected to public office in Daytona. She was also successfully re-elected to the position of mayor at the age of 79, making her the oldest mayor in Daytona's history. I was forever changed by Yvonne's selfless passion and drive to challenge others to be the best that they could be, no matter how rocky their start may have been.

When I signed my second NFL contract with the Jacksonville Jaguars, I had just finished my last final at Bethune-Cookman. Of course I called everyone who was important to me and Yvonne was at the top of that list. As I explained to her my great news, she said, "oh that's wonderful Stevie, but are your finals over? And how did you do on them? And you promised that you were going to come over and clean this garage, so before you leave for Jacksonville, I expect that to be taken care of. Love you!" and then she hung up. The biggest news of my life and she was asking me when I was going to clean the garage?! I laugh about it now because that to me exemplifies the definition of true Family. People holding you accountable to a higher standard. Family does not only include those related to you by blood. Maybe it's your best friend of 20 years, an old Family friend that you call your aunt, your college mentor, or even your current boss. Family to me is anyone that inspires you to break out of your comfort zone, ditch the excuses, and be the best you that you can possibly be. Just like Yvonne spent her life doing. Being Greater Than The Game means surrounding yourself with teammates that lift you up, not break you down. I often find new members to include in my definition of Family, most of them in unlikely places, spanning all different ages, Faiths, genders and races. We definitely can't succeed in the journey alone, and positioning yourself to be encouraged by people who are truly in your corner is one of the most important ways that we can change the things about our past that aren't serving our present.

I have always wondered what it would be like to go back in time like Michael J. Fox did in Back To The Future II. But then I got to thinking, my past and my Family is a major part of who I am today, and I wouldn't change anything about it. I used the struggles and disappointments from my Family history as encouragement to change certain negative circumstances that plagued my Family and to drive my present decisions which will ultimately shape the future that I am cultivating right now. Each one of us has that power. Again we are back to the incredible power of choice. We have the power to surround ourselves with Family that doesn't let you say, "there's nothing I can do about that". Because there is always something you can do about it. Just go ahead and start, and you will quickly become a leader in your own Greater Than The Game story. Like Yvonne, I believe that true leaders create other leaders, not more followers.

"Stevie has been challenged at every
level on and off the field and every
time he has stepped up to the challenge
and he never doubted the gifts that
God gave him he loved the game of
football but saw the true value in the
game of life as a player and coach
I have never seen anyone play the
DE/OLB position better than
Stevie Baggs yes even
Lawrence Taylor"

Coach C.A. Wyatt
Bethune-Cookman University

CHAPTER 3

FOCUS

"Why have perfect eyesight but no vision"

Life is busy. Balancing school, work, Family, exercise, volunteer commitments, social engagements and all those other things that come up during the day can be exhausting. Too often, we are simply going through the motions just to get everything done. And even then, it seems like there just aren't enough hours in the day to do what we need in order to feel any sense of accomplishment. And then it starts all over again tomorrow. In the blink of an eye the week is done and all of those tasks that were priorities on Monday get pushed to next week, next month, or next year. Sometimes, they are forgotten altogether and the failure to address them in a meaningful way can lead to unnecessary anxiety and stress. Have you ever noticed that when you put something off because it seems too difficult or overwhelming at the time, that same undertaking becomes ten times more difficult later on? That's because not having a proper plan of action to deal with the task or emotion creates negative energy towards it and in turn contributes to the rapid decline of the ability to promptly and appropriately deal with whatever it is that faces you. So how do we fix this common problem in our lives? I believe that the answer lies buried deep within one word: Focus.

Now, this Focus thing is much easier said than done in my opinion. There is a distraction waiting for us at every turn. Focus on making a healthy meal and the phone rings. An hour later, there is no time to cook and the choice suddenly becomes, "do I go to Chick-fil-A or McDonalds". So quickly we are lead in the opposite direction of where we intend to be because we have failed on the basic primary goal to Focus on what needs to be done in the present moment. We are all guilty of spending so much time living in the future (and past) that we cannot appreciate what is in front of us right now. Focus requires the commitment and intention to be fully present in our goals, tasks, emotions and relationships and the ability to recognize that which does not serve us in reaching our targeted actions.

While I wholeheartedly believe that properly applying genuine Focus to any situation is multifaceted, we have to start somewhere. That somewhere in my opinion is setting up that Focus, for both short and long term endeavors, in a logical and clear way. What better way to do that than to make a list! We make grocery lists so that we don't forget what is missing in the refrigerator, guest lists so that we know who will be attending a party, and basic to-do lists so that we can prioritize our day at work. Why then, are we generally opposed to making other types of lists? I know that lists can be seen as negative in some instances, and people who make lists may be considered obsessive or neurotic. I don't necessarily believe that. The majority of people I know who are driven by making lists are Focused, attentive and purposeful in action, traits that most of us could probably learn and benefit from.

Growing up, my mother always reinforced the importance of being a leader and not being tricked into just going along with the crowd. Succeeding at this meant having specific and individual goals which required a lot of time and attention from me. Or, in other words, maintaining Focus. By the time I was in my senior year in high school, I was very good at identifying those things that were required in my life to get me to the next level. The problem was, one day I knew what I wanted and needed to do in order that a certain task be accomplished, but then a week later, I was back at square one. So I decided to try something very simple: I wrote it down. I wrote down exactly what I wanted to accomplish, clearly and with intention. I then made the list plainly visible because it certainly wouldn't have done any good tucked away in a drawer that I opened on occasion. There it was, in big writing, taped to my ceiling. Every night before I went to bed I looked at the list, and every morning that list was the first thing that I laid my eyes on. I had no choice but to internalize and Focus on each word because it was always right in front of my face. There was absolutely no escaping what I had set out to do. In case you were wondering, my personal goals at that time were as follows: 1) Cultivate a closer relationship with

God; 2) Love, honor and respect my Family; 3) Make honor roll; 4) Be named as the team captain of the Football team; 5) Make first team all-State; and 6) Earn a full scholarship to a Division-1 College/University (Florida State University to be exact). I was never more Focused on anything in my life than I was on those goals, and my life absolutely changed that year. Not only did I feel closer to God than ever before, my relationships with my Family members transformed in ways I could only dream. I made honor roll, was the captain of the Football team and was named to the Florida all-State team. The only thing that I didn't quite manage was that full scholarship to the Division-1 school. I was offered a walk-on opportunity at Florida State, but at the time, my Financial situation didn't allow me to pursue that. While it was not necessarily my first choice, my full-scholarship to Bethune-Cookman, a Division II school, was exactly where I needed to be to pursue my Football dream, and more importantly, to learn the many life-lessons that those four years taught me. So looking back, I not only fulfilled my goals, but exceeded them. And to think, it was all because I chose to take that one tiny extra step in putting my goals into print. Our dreams and aspirations, objectives and ambitions write our personal life story, so why shouldn't they be published. The special story that we personally write every day requires our full attention and Focus. When we can actually see what it is that drives and motivates us, we can be penetrated to the core and channel that Focus into tangible results.

If you have ever attended a yoga or meditation class, you are aware that the focal point is most often "being mindfully present". What does that actually mean? I used to think it just sounded crazy. Aren't we always living in the present just by virtue of being alive? The answer is most definitely not. When you are laying on that yoga mat trying to Focus on just being in the room, the last thing that your mind will do on its own is Focus on being at rest. You think about your shopping list, and a friend's problem, and what you need to do in the seconds just after you leave the room, and what your dog is doing. It is one of the most difficult things in the entire world to just be at peace in mind and body and to Focus on that present moment. Successful Focus requires being present within the fabric of our goals and that presence is the most challenging aspect of true Focus. At least for me anyway. Most goals, objectives, ambitions require multiple steps and overlooking those small things that may seem trivial on the way to the ultimate prize is extremely easy. The problem is, the small or regular tasks that we gloss over may make or break the final goal. The worst part is that you don't even realize that it is happening until it is far too late. Use the present to plan and amend goals while in the process of achievement and do not Focus too far into the future or you may find things fall off track very easily. I should know...

In late spring, 2004, Bethune-Cookman held its annual Pro Day where Football players such as myself were able to showcase our talents in advance of that year's NFL Draft. Given my record-breaking senior season, I was likely one of the main attractions for any professional scouts who would be making the trip to Florida. The only thing was, I wasn't actually there. I was at home. "Resting". It wasn't that I didn't want to be there, because that would have gone directly against my seize-the-day mentality. Instead, I was advised by my agent not to attend Pro Day because I had just recently pulled my hamstring muscle. He unequivocally told me that I was "guaranteed" to get drafted by a team and further advised me that I should just take a rain check on Pro Day. That way, he said, I wouldn't risk running a sub-par 40-yard dash time. The decision was purely precautionary. The doctor didn't tell me I shouldn't attend, and even so, as every Football player will tell you, I played through and survived much worse pain and injury before. If I was going to be drafted, what was the point? I trusted him, and I took his advice and stayed home. Well, this trivial step (or misstep as I soon found out) in fulfilling my NFL dream may have single-handedly altered my entire career. I should have known that the text messages and calls from my bewildered teammates asking where the heck I was that day were foreshadowing something that I couldn't quite wrap my head around.

NFL Draft Day 2004. This was my time. Every practice, game, and workout that my body and mind endured in the past 7 years culminated at this 2-day peak. My agent had told me that I would undoubtedly be drafted in the 3rd round of the Draft, if not higher. And he didn't use the word "might". It was a given. An absolute certainty. I felt like my entire Football future rested on what would unfold in the next 48 hours and I was beyond excited for the moment that my name would be called out on the television screen. My Family held a two-day party for me in Miami, and I invited many of close friends and Family to share in my joy. Day one of the Draft went by and I didn't hear my name, but that just energized me even more for day two. I could barely contain myself as my Family gathered at my grandmother's home. Watching. Waiting. But as each round was completed, my heart started to sink a little more. Until I found myself alone in the bedroom late that evening, down on my knees, wondering what had just happened. My "absolute certainty" in getting drafted turned into my "absolute nightmare" as my name didn't get called at any point during those two days. I didn't get drafted. Point blank. Period.

I liken my Draft Day story to that of a bride. She wouldn't start planning her wedding before she was engaged. Or at least she wouldn't pay for a venue and flowers and a dress and send out invitations without some evidence (a ring maybe?) that the wedding day was actually going to happen. In my mind, I knew I was going to be drafted like I knew the sun would rise the following morning. But besides the empty words of my agent, looking back I really couldn't be sure. I didn't have concrete proof and as much as I relied on my Faith in those moments leading up to the Draft, there really was no telling what would actually develop. On my proverbial wedding day, however, as I stood at the end of the aisle waiting for my true love to walk through the doors of the church, on the threshold of beginning a new and joyous phase of life together, my bride got cold feet. I stood alone at the altar. Alone. Speechless. Broken-hearted. I got ahead of myself. I didn't Focus on the immediate goal in front of me, in the present moment. I missed my Pro Day and instead of rescheduling or somehow ensuring that I got enough face time with NFL scouts, I planned myself a party for something that ultimately did not come to fruition. Instead of maintaining the necessary Focus on each equally important step along the way, I skipped all the stuff that I thought was meaningless. Or at least that wouldn't really make a meaningful difference to the end goal. I threw myself a wedding, but I didn't have a bride. Lack of Focus lead me down the dangerous path of passing over the right now and solely concentrating on the outcome.

It took me many years to come to terms with what I now refer to as my "Draft Day Disaster"; however, I can now say without hesitation that I make certain that

I Focus on each and every step that is necessary to whatever it is that I am trying to accomplish. There are no minor or insignificant moves what it comes to our personal goals. Each phase brings us closer, but neglecting one of those phases because it seems like it doesn't really matter, can prove extraordinarily detrimental if we do not Focus wholeheartedly on the present steps. Like I said, I should know how it feels to skip the engagement and go straight to the wedding, and I have lived and learned from those demoralizing consequences. Set yourself up for success in reaching your goals by Focusing on the present moment as your most important moment.

Many of our goals and aspirations are quite personal and it is unlikely we want share the entire journey with other people. Take any objectives that relate to personal growth as an example: we just don't share every single thing that happens in our lives with the whole world. Other goals however, may be facilitated by the assistance and input of certain third parties. Some may even require other people to ensure that the goal succeeds. I have learned that the majority of our ambitions can furthered by those persons who have our best interests at heart, but more importantly, those that are Focused on the same dreams. When we align our Focus with like-minded individuals, we increase the chance of meeting, exceeding and changing our game immensely. Say for example, your goal is to be accepted at Harvard University Law School. It is unlikely you would discuss the application process with a friend whose goal is to be accepted at Yale University Medical School. Both equally prestigious institutions, yet two very different roads to get there. Focusing on and conquering each step toward the common goal is what makes it imperative that we surround ourselves with people who can motivate us and push us further. Perhaps even more poignant is the team goal, where more than one person actually wants the exact same result. It is here that collective Focus turns dreams into reality.

I am privileged to have been a member of one Super Bowl team and three Grey Cup (the CFL equivalent of the Super Bowl) teams over the course of my Football career. I can say without any reservation that a single characteristic defined each one of those teams over the course of the season leading up to the final game: shared Focus. At the beginning of training camp, every single one of my teammates, coaches, trainers and staff wanted to play for the championship. Everything we did prepared us to reach that goal. The offense was Focused. The defense was Focused. The team was Focused. We never wavered in that Focus and ultimately, we got to each respective championship game because we did it together. Had there been even one small element of the team that lacked the required Focus, our season would have ended much earlier.

On paper, the 2009 CFL season was undoubtedly my personal best. At season's end I lead the league in the quarterback sack and tackles for loss categories. Over the season I collected defensive player of the week honors 5 times, and I was defensive player of the league for the month of August. Those accolades, however, were just a brief pause in the ultimate team journey to the Grey Cup. Throughout the season my defensive teammates and I Focused on our mantra, "effort is the edge" with the practical goal of creating turnovers, limiting penalties, and flipping field position so that our offence could score more easily. Sounds simple, but we Focused as a team and as a unit daily on those principles from preseason, during every practice, through the playoffs, and to the Grey Cup. We made it to the final assent of our mountain top because we aligned and cultivated the Focus necessary to reach the pinnacle of the CFL season. Imagine this: Grey Cup, fourth quarter, up by 2 points, our defense holds the opposing team's offense to a long field goal attempt on the final play of the game, just like we had Focused on all season long. The kick went up, and went wide. They missed the attempt and we won the championship! And we all lived happily ever after, admiring our 2009 Grey Cup rings. I truly wish that was the end of the story. As we were celebrating our victory, however, the realization that there was a penalty flag laying silently on the field near the field goal formation crept over all of us. As the referee turned on his microphone, I had a sinking feeling that this wasn't going to be good news. Well it sure wasn't. Turns out that we had one too many players on the field for that final field goal attempt. The result was a do-over, and the kicker wasn't going to miss twice. He nailed it. And simultaneously drove a nail straight into the hearts of all of us. The championship was ours for the taking, but we didn't Focus on that other common goal, limiting penalties. There is not one specific person to blame for what happened that late November night. It was a team effort and just as we had done all season, we lived and died together on that field. That day, I know that a little piece of each of us was left out there with that penalty flag. The heartbreak I felt however, does not surpasses the immense sense of accomplishment that I felt throughout that season as a part of a team with common goals, shared ambitions and group Focus. I wouldn't trade those successes for the world.

Focus is a crucial aspect of any journey towards becoming Greater than the Game. It is a skill that requires great effort, determination, and a plan of action so that it can be successfully implemented to assist us in the daily task of improving our game. I honestly believe that Focus can transform dreams into reality, ambition into accomplishment, and life ordinary into life extraordinary. The first step is organizing that Focus into a concrete set of visible aspirations. Only when we see them in writing on a daily basis do these aspirations have a higher rate of achievement. That may be the easy part though, because the most difficult aspect of Focus, in my opinion, is making sure that we don't lose sight of the here and now. Hindsight is 20/20, and living with the consequences of "what could have been if only I had [fill in the blank] . . ." can be debilitating when trying to rebound from negative events in life. I am sure that you have heard the saying "it's the journey, not the destination" that teaches us the most. Sure it would have been fantastic to win the Grey Cup, or a Super Bowl, but if I only chose to Focus on the pain of the loss, I couldn't have grown positively from the experiences. Write it down, be mindful of it, and take someone who shares it with you along for the ride. Watch as Focus directs your path to becoming Greater Than The Game and ensures that you don't miss anything important along the way.

CHAPTER 4

FINANCES

"If your worth is based on your bank account
or your occupation, you will always be broke"

I could probably write an entire book on my relationship with money. At times in my life, I made some really, really stupid decisions based solely on my Finances. What I learned however, is that to be truly Financially free, money (or lack thereof) absolutely and unequivocally cannot dictate every move that you make. Finances cannot just translate to money. Given that a vast number of personal and relationship issues can seemingly be directly attributed to money (again, or lack thereof), I know that this may fall on deaf ears. But please hear me out. I don't need to say that money is a requirement to live, eat, travel, enjoy hobbies etc. That's a given; however, it's ultimately how we act and react to money that actually determines our level of happiness. Have you ever said to yourself, "if I could just buy 'x' I would be so happy." Or, "if I could just afford 'y' we would not have these problems." Well I would be willing to bet that even when you finally bought 'x' and could finally afford 'y' you were not any happier and the problems didn't just disappear. At least not in the long run. It is very easy to receive a short term benefit or a fleeting sense of euphoria when purchasing something beautiful and new and shiny and coveted. The problem is, that we as human beings are programmed to be unsatisfied with material wealth because we will always want more. The used car isn't good enough; then the brand new domestic car isn't good enough; then the over-priced import isn't good enough. That said, there is an underlying motivator as to why the car that was just fine two years ago, isn't fine anymore. Maybe it's because your Family has grown and the car is too small (a positive motivator). Or maybe it's because your coworker bought a new car and you can't possibly be upstaged by him (a negative motivator). Money on the surface may appear to be at issue in every aspect of our lives, but more often than not, that Financial angle is actually masking a deeper issue. It is up to us to recognize and evaluate what that issue might be. Is it positive or negative? Will giving into the desire to spend money or buy something on credit help us or hurt us? Giving money the exclusive power to dictate happiness takes all of the positive benefits of money (and yes, there are many), and turns them around tenfold in the negative, manifesting as problems that plague us daily. And then to top it off, we act as if we have no idea where those problems arose. Like all things, just be honest with yourself. If you are feeling any negativity towards your Finances, I assure you that the motivating factor behind a lot of the stuff that you purchased to cause those feelings was negative: perhaps you gave into a 'want' and not a 'need'. I know that you have all looked at someone who has more material wealth than you and thought, "if I had just half that much money there is no way I would look and act so miserable" (don't deny it, we have all done it on multiple occasions). What you don't immediately realize is the life cost (time spent, relationship health, moral cost, credit card debt, mental strength) to that person. There has to be a reason, or a lot of reasons, for that miserable look on someone's face, and it's certainly not because he or she has a large bank account. Sometimes that life cost far outweighs the momentary joy that a material purchase will bring. Am I saying that all wealthy people are unhappy? Absolutely not. At the end of the day it is the attitude, reaction, and relationship with Finances that will determine whether someone actually "has it all", or just has some expensive things.

Many challenges arise daily between teammates, as coworkers, on a professional Football team. Given that I have experienced both the locker room as an office, and a corporate setting as an office, I can attest to the fact that the challenges are quite unique with respect to the Football context. Primarily, all of your coworkers are male, generously paid (according to the general public), and share bold character traits that can manifest in some very destructive ways. Most notably, competition is rampant. A healthy dose of competition of course allows each player to realize his full potential when it comes to doing his respective job on the field and that is obviously a very good thing. On the other hand, when competition drives certain behavior away from the Football field, things can start to get a little bit more complicated.

As a simple example, imagine that behind every starter on a Football team, there are at least one or two reserve players who see a lot less (or no) playing time each Sunday. Some Football players will spend their entire career backing up a starter. And sometimes the starter will change, but that backup position player never gets the chance to showcase his skills. Likewise, a starter can just as easily lose their position rank to a backup player. That said, it doesn't matter if you are a long-serving veteran, or a rookie who was just drafted, it is important to remember that loyalty in Football only lasts as long as your last good play. I am sure you have probably heard the saying "Any Given Sunday". Well it's the absolute truth because any feasible change can happen to a Football roster from week to week depending on team and individual performances. So what happens when there is a major shift in hierarchy, especially when a long serving veteran is displaced from the position that he has dedicated himself to excelling at for the majority of his life. Players cannot control what the coaches, management and ownership decide from the perspective of the team and in situations like these, there are common feelings of anger, resentment and intense bitterness directed towards the teammate who essentially stole your job. It is at this moment that unhealthy competition can begin. The best example I can think of is the age old "Keeping up with the Joneses" story. A teammate buys a piece of jewelry. In order to show that he has a larger contract, another teammate buys a bigger piece. And another, yet a bigger one. Until there are so many diamonds being flashed around that you would think that you were on the set of a hip-hop video. The same thing happens with shoes, and clothes, and cars, and houses, and bar tabs, and anything else you could possibly think of. I am the first to say that it feels nice to reward yourself and your Family to celebrate the accomplishment of a major goal, but it is the motivation behind these purchases that can be problematic. The feelings of one-upmanship and delusions of grandeur which drive these decisions are what makes them so dangerous. A rookie who has just entered the professional ranks may think that he has a lot of money to spend, and compared to what he had in college, that could very well be true. But when you evaluate everything surrounding that first contract, it may not be that simple. Firstly, the average career in the NFL, or any professional sport for that matter, is extraordinarily short as compared with a 'normal' career. Secondly, there are so many risk factors in connection with the job, including but not limited to the fact that most of the contract money is not guaranteed, the player may very well be living in a here today, gone tomorrow type of situation. And we all know that just as quickly as money comes, it goes.

I fell into this trap more times than I would like to admit. I looked at players and thought, I am better than them, why are they playing and I am not. So I made unwise purchases, did unwise things with my money, just to keep up appearances. To show the rest of the world that I was a Football player and I had made it. To prove to myself that I had made it. But I soon realized that I couldn't keep up. I couldn't pay for the repairs on the import SUV so I was forced to sell, and I couldn't make mortgage payments on the condo so it eventually went into foreclosure. I needed a vehicle, and I needed a place to live. It was the motivation behind what I bought and where I bought it that lacked any sort of sensibility and responsibility. I was making purchases that went well beyond my Financial means and I learned the hard way that everything can be taken away in the blink of an eye. I urge you to use this story to think about your own situation when it comes to Finances. Sometimes happiness actually means saying no to purchases that will inflict Financial burden on you. And I can certainly attest to the fact that fancy clothes and fancy cars do not equate to contentment. These material items might give you a very temporary thrill, but making sound Financial decisions that are best for you in your personal circumstances will allow you to remain accountable to yourself. You can't blame anyone else when you find yourself paying for something that you really couldn't afford just because you had to impress someone. There are so many non-tangible gifts that each of us can share with others to show our self-worth that don't cost a cent – love, friendship, understanding, knowledge – and I believe that these qualities are infinitely more valuable than enormous Financial wealth. And I can almost guarantee that when it comes time to pay the credit card bills or loan payments, the Family, friends and coworkers that you were desperately trying to impress won't be there to bail you out of a bad situation.

Summer 2008. I had been bouncing around the CFL and AFL and didn't really have anywhere to call home in a Football context, so I went back to Atlanta and decided that I needed to do something to keep me sane. Anything. Growing up in the church, and relying heavily on my Faith, I had always heard the message, "we must be mission-minded, not just money-minded". I could certainly appreciate the sentiment, and I always had a desire to give back to the community, but I didn't really know how to practically accomplish that given my current circumstances. The thing was, I didn't have anything to give back except my time. My paycheck wasn't enough to even cover my basic human needs, so I certainly couldn't donate a huge sum of money to a worthy cause even if I wanted to. Financially that would have been impossible for me at the time. You can't give what you don't have, even if it's to the most amazing cause in the entire world. Remember that. But just because you cannot make a Financial contribution, doesn't mean that you should sit around and do nothing! You can get involved in a million other ways. With the assistance of some of my former teammates, friends and Family who were motivated by a similar desire to use their knowledge and skills to benefit the community, I created a youth Football camp and life skills clinic. We didn't have a large budget, but we had people who were willing to spend their valuable time bringing the vision to fruition. Think about the phrases "spending your time", and "time is money", and you will understand that time is just as, if not more valuable in some instances, than money. Sure it's nice to be able to donate money, but donating an investment of time, those hours, minutes and days that you can never ever get refunded, can make a world of difference. Reflect on the time you have invested in friendships, relationships, the cause that you hold close to your heart, and you should realize that you are making a Financial contribution without ever opening your wallet. The time that was donated to that Football camp couldn't have been valuated in a monetary context, even if we tried. Imagine the collective years of training, education and leadership provided by my teammates to the children who had never met a professional Football player, let alone spent the day with one! Putting a dollar value on the knowledge that we all readily shared with the camp attendees seems trivial. The experience in and of itself was rewarding, humbling, and totally satisfying and I expect that everyone involved in making that day a success would agree with me but the most remarkable part? Not one of us came home from that camp even one penny richer.

This 2008 Football camp and life skills clinic is only one of the countless events that I have been a part of organizing or attended as a guest, but it resonates with me for a particularly special reason. At the time, my aunt was living with a diagnosis of terminal pancreatic cancer. The doctors had done everything they could, and she was living on borrowed time. To many, this type of diagnosis would be enough to totally check out of life. And with good reason. She was in pain every second of the day, but the thing about my aunt was, you couldn't tell by the look on her face. She always wore a smile that could light up a room. On top of that, she was my biggest supporter in ensuring this camp went smoothly: running around picking up supplies, ensuring sponsors were on board, helping with registration and volunteer placement. If you didn't personally know what she was dealing with, you certainly wouldn't have been able to see the torture her body was under by the way she was carrying herself. She wasn't worrying about the inevitable, she was spending the most valuable time of her life helping others. You absolutely can't put a price on that. While there is no quantitative number to attach to my aunt's work, the Financial benefit was immeasurable nonetheless. If the camp touched just one child, to make once positive change in his or her life, the value is priceless. And I can assure you that more than one child was impacted that day. To me, this is far more fulfilling and more precious than any type of monetary success. Making money is usually very personal, whereas engaging in a life of service makes limitless connections with those people who truly need our help at a certain time in their lives. No one will remember how many quarterback sacks I had during my career, or how many interceptions my teammate made over the course of his, but the children impacted at that camp because of the time invested in them will remember the experience forever. This call to service is my late aunt's legacy and this camp was the first time I really and truly believed in Football as more than just a game played on the field or as a way to earn an income to support myself and my Family. For the first time I was truly able to comprehend that my purpose was Greater Than The Game.

In an ideal world, I would volunteer all of my time for whatever worthy cause I could find. I would spend my life pursuing philanthropic endeavors. The only problem is that like everybody else, I have bills to pay. It is not feasible to simply donate all of your time and not actually make a living. That would be irresponsible and would go directly against good Financial health, placing unnecessary burdens and stresses on you. Just as you cannot make Financial contributions if you don't have the money, similarly you cannot donate time that you do not have to give. There must be a balance kept between wanting to do the right thing for a greater cause, and making sure that whatever you are doing is within your means. I think this is where the majority of us run into great difficulty. How many times have you taken a job for the sole reason that you are in immediate need of money (read here: desperate). I know that I have done so more times that I care to remember. Sometimes, that job may really be the only option at the moment. But when that is the only option, I ask you to think beyond the pay check. Are you using the position as a stepping stone to move up in a company? Is the job fulfilling you in ways that go beyond Finances? If not, are you actively seeking alternate employment? If you answered no to all of these questions, then I encourage you to seriously consider if that pay check is worth the personal sacrifice that you are making. Doing it "just for the money" seems pretty empty, no matter how many zeros are at the end of your salary. Now don't get me wrong here, I certainly do not mean that you should sit around and wait for the most perfect job to fall from the sky. Running away from reality catches up quickly when we start living in a fantasy world, but I mean think beyond just the Financial benefit of that job. Maybe you have a great relationship with your coworkers, or the position has opened doors for you in other avenues of life that are important to you. How is that job furthering your game or at least assisting in the elevation of your game? Those minimum wage jobs that I took to make ends meet while I was actively pursuing my Football career weren't necessarily my dream jobs, but they were nonetheless imperative to my ability to chase my dream. Without them, I couldn't have continued training, I wouldn't have been able to travel for potential meetings and tryouts, and I certainly wouldn't have been able to pursue Football for as long as I did. Most importantly, I learned a lot about myself when I sincerely opened up to the positive aspects of each job and I realized this: while you are pursuing your passion, you actually figure out your purpose. Simple. Profound. Life changing.

I wholeheartedly believe that pursuing my passion in Football has lead me to my ultimate life purpose in co-founding and running the non-profit foundation C.E.T.A [Creating Empowerment Through Autonomy]. Remember when I said if given the chance I would live a life of philanthropic endeavors? I believe that Football, my recent acting opportunities (which resulted from connections that I have made throughout the Football years), and ultimately this book, Greater Than The Game, allows me to actually realize that purpose. All of the other pieces of the puzzle have lead to this: the ability to reach the unreachable population through the meaning and activities of C.E.T.A. Spreading the message that empowerment eliminates dependency and Focusing on breaking the generational and Familial setbacks in economically challenged communities is what is at the very core of my being. Without Football, my passion, I may never have been lead to follow through with C.E.T.A., my purpose. All of the principles that I speak about in this book are actively visible through C.E.T.A.'s tireless work in the community and it is my heartfelt belief that this is only the beginning for us as an organization. We have only scratched the surface of C.E.T.A.'s reach because I have made a conscious decision that each future opportunity I choose to engage in, to spend my time with, will support C.E.T.A.'s efforts. Directly or indirectly.

I am blessed at this time in my life to know exactly what I have been called to do, and I know not everyone is able to say the same. What I can share with you, however, is that if you truly use every chance available to pursue your passion, whether it be through a job, through a volunteer position, or by Focusing on the requisite steps to realize your dream, you too will find that purpose. I guarantee it, and maybe it will be even sooner than you think! The crazy part about experiencing that breakthrough is that all those Financial issues you found yourself worrying about? They miraculously disappear. The road on which your purpose lies is paved with opportunities that are beyond your wildest imagination. Those temporary jobs that you "had to take" to get through the week will just be a distant memory. Keep an open mind and don't let anyone discourage you from following your dreams and passions. I can attest to the fact that forging along that long and sometimes very difficult path, investing time in yourself and into your dreams, will guide your game to its pinnacle.

What I want you to take from this chapter is very simple: good Finances do not necessarily equate to a having a large bank account. Similarly, being rich doesn't just mean taking home a hefty pay check. Investing time in relationships and worthy causes has a much greater return on investment than spending your day at a job counting down the hours until you can punch out, just to go home and do it all over again tomorrow. When you couple that investment with relationships and causes that are directly in line with your passion, and you make intelligent choices with the Financial means that are at your disposal at this point in time, you will be absolutely unstoppable. I assure you. The worry of having enough money to survive will fade and you will soon have more resources at your fingertips than you will know what to do with. Pursuing your passion and ultimately finding that elusive purpose is the only way that you will experience absolute Financial bliss: that point where enough becomes all you could ever want; money, happiness, fulfillment. Anything you can possibly dream of will be right there in your midst. Money can define your game, but true Financial success will facilitate your Greater Than The Game life.

"'Mr. Determined' you always stayed focused on reaching your goals no matter what the obstacle was in your career. Never Quitting until you reached the mountain top of that goal."

Barrin Simpson
CFL Hall of Fame

CHAPTER 5

FITNESS

"Your overall wellness is directly attributable to your combined social, economic, physical, mental, and spiritual wellbeing; true wealth is health!"

I have spent a large portion of my life figuring out exactly how to maximize my training regimen so that my body would be in top physical shape, ready to play Football at a professional level at any given moment when the opportunity presented itself. Although I am no longer actively pursuing Football as a career, I remain wholly dedicated to my body, fine-tuning it daily through various types of physical Fitness activities. It would be very easy to devote this entire chapter to physical Fitness given that it goes hand in hand with my passion for Football; however, I believe that the Fitness concept is much more profound. Please don't get me wrong here, physical Fitness is very much an integral part of the collective Fitness model, and I will certainly highlight its importance throughout this section. Just think, if we don't have a healthy working vessel (our body), we cannot even think about moving to the other pieces of the Fitness puzzle. That said, there are other equally important parts to consider when assessing your overall Fitness level.

What exactly does a collective Fitness model entail you ask? The answer to that question actually lies within the mission statement and culminates in the activities of the C.E.T.A. Foundation. We at C.E.T.A. believe that peak Fitness is realized when one's physical, social, spiritual, mental and economic well-being are working together in perfect harmony. Ok, now I know that this sounds like a far-reaching concept, but I sincerely believe that each piece is inextricably tied to the other. C.E.T.A.'s activities are designed to promote each of these individual pieces of Fitness, while at the same time encouraging the inclusive view that without one, the other will not work at its climax. Let's take a simple example, one that many of us are familiar with: in order to have a good workout, you must fuel your body with the right nutrients. In order to have access to the right food and vitamins, you need to be in a Financial position to purchase fresh fruits, vegetables, lean meats etc. Being Financially Fit supports the personal quest to physical Fitness. The collective Fitness model teaches us that success in one aspect of Fitness will encourage success in another, and vice versa. When I really started to think about it, I realized that Fitness is really just a review of everything that we have examined in the preceding chapters: Family (social Fitness) + Faith (spiritual Fitness) + Focus (mental Fitness) + Finances (economic Fitness) + Fitness (physical Fitness) = total Fitness. It is at this total Fitness pinnacle, however, that we truly see how becoming Greater Than The Game is more than a sum of its parts – it's a lifelong commitment to developing and strengthening all of the parts to operate as one perfect working unit.

"I should workout." "I should join a gym." "I should go for a walk." "I could really stand to lose 5 pounds." Sound familiar? We have all done it. And why didn't you workout, get to the gym, go for the walk, lose the weight? Excuses. We all have excuses, it's just that some of us are better at giving in to them. We are all busy. So if you're going to come with that excuse, you are going to have to do a lot better at selling me on the reason that you are not spending time investing in your body. I cannot even begin to imagine all of the money that big Fitness establishments are bringing in from clients that have set foot in the gym once – the day that they activated their membership. Right here we have a perfect example of Finances intersecting with Fitness. If you know that you are really and truly not going to use the membership, don't sign up. Do you really have money to literally throw away? For some, the gym setting is intimidating and causes anxiety. That's OK! There are a million and one other ways to stay active, it's just a matter of finding the right fit for you. Start walking, ride a bike, go for a hike, take a yoga class. But I will not accept excuses. Physical Fitness is one of the F's that is non-negotiable for me. You absolutely must take care of your precious body because as I previously stated, without it nothing is possible. How can you be Greater Than The Game if you are always tired, or sick, or cannot move around easily. Not going to happen! I am not saying that you need to become an Olympic athlete overnight. No. I want you to do something. Anything. Because starting a physical Fitness regimen is never a waste of time, but believing in all of those reasons you can't do it, is. And I promise you that just taking the first step is the biggest hurdle. Think back for a moment to our conversation about Focus and use those tools to help you in taking the initial leap: write down your Fitness goals; celebrate and reward yourself for sticking to, reaching, and exceeding those goals; join a group of individuals who have similar goals and draw motivation from each other. "But I'm just too tired today, I will do it tomorrow." All we have is right now and if you don't use the present moment to make a conscious decision to change, your Fitness will keep getting pushed aside for more "important" things. I cannot reiterate enough there is nothing as important as your health! Make it a priority! I implore you to seriously consider if your excuses are really good enough to compromise your Fitness and your health.

I know a little something about physical inability and excuses when it comes to my performance on the Football field. I was born pigeon-toed and walk bowlegged. If you have ever seen me in person or watched a game that I played in, you will have immediately noticed my abnormal gait. I can assure you that every media commentator, every newspaper columnist and every coach and teammate has not only noticed, but commented and made assumptions about my ability because of this physical characteristic. I have never known anything different, so I made a decision very early on in my life that I would never let being pigeon-toed interfere with what I wanted to accomplish. First we were told that I would grow out of it. When that didn't happen, doctors told us that I could have surgery to attempt the correction of my hip placement, but there were a lot of potential issues that just didn't seem to be worth the risk. So, I learned to live with my funny walk. Everyone else just can't let it go! My teammates even went so far as to call me "crazy legs", one of the nicknames that I have never really cared all too much for. As I was pursuing my NFL dream, my agent said something which has always stuck with me: "People are not looking for reasons to keep you Stevie, they are looking for reasons to eliminate you". This statement goes far beyond the Football context and extends into daily tasks. Everyone does not want to see you succeed. There are naysayers and excuses waiting at every turn. All of the records, stats and accolades didn't matter at this point. For some reason, coaches and managers didn't think I could make it in the NFL. It would have been very easy at this point to look at the logistics of my unorthodox foot placement and place blame squarely right there. Maybe they were scared, maybe they didn't think that I was worth the risk because of the way that I ran. But I absolutely and unequivocally refuse to buy into that explanation entirely. I proved them wrong in high school, I proved them wrong in college, and I went on to prove them wrong in the professional Football realm when I was given the opportunity.

I look at it this way: had I not been forced to overcome this physical abnormality, maybe I wouldn't have worked as hard on my Fitness. Or maybe I wouldn't have had the drive and determination to continue pursing Football when they told me no, over and over and over again. I choose to celebrate being pigeon-toed, instead of using it as any sort of justification as to why things didn't turn out exactly how I had planned. Maybe I would even go so far as to say that it is one of the major reasons that I even played Football as long as I actually did. It was the motivation and fire I needed to keep going when all of the odds were stacked against me. When someone tries to dampen your spirit, I encourage you to use their rationalization as to why you can't, as motivation to do even more. No matter what sort of insults are thrown at you, no matter how difficult the obstacle may seem, nothing can stop you from attaining your Fitness goals (and any goals) if you believe in yourself. Invest in your health through Fitness activities that you enjoy and make today the day that your body becomes the catalyst for your Greater Than The Game lifestyle.

We are living in a society where the food that we put on the table is under constant scrutiny. Non-GMO's, organic, reduced sugar, gluten-free, whole grains, who can even keep up with all of the new lingo! The truth is, there will always be a newer and better way to lose weight and stay healthy with the help of the foods we choose to consume. That is the beauty of research and education. The problem is that the majority of the information that we passively receive is through advertisements and media reporting. And these are the exact same entities that have a financial interest in providing that information. Trust me, most companies are not promoting healthy eating because they care even one bit about your health.

They care about the bottom line. Finances rule the day and if we are not careful, it is very easy to become consumed by that get healthy quick mentality. Perhaps even more dangerous are the conclusions that we draw in equating certain concepts. *Organic* sugar does not mean that all of a sudden, sugar miraculously becomes healthy. I do not purport to be an expert in nutrition and I will not spend any time telling you what you should and shouldn't eat. My message here is very simple: when you know better, you do better. When you take an active interest in educating yourself about the products that you are consuming, you may find that it is relatively easy to start making better choices. And that's what it is all about, taking that first step in taking control of your personal health and Fitness.

As I have alluded to throughout this book, there have been times that Financially I did not know how I was going to pay for my next meal. It was at these times that I realized why there is an obesity epidemic plaguing our society. This is certainly not a novel concept, but I really felt it in my life at these moments when I was really struggling. Fast food, or in other words, non-healthy food is so much cheaper than wholesome food. Point blank. I ate McDonalds cheeseburgers because I could afford them and it was convenient and quick. I used to wonder why I saw low-income families in fast food restaurants all of the time, and I know that the reason is twofold: 1) it's cheap; and 2) they just don't know any better. There are countless studies on the correlation between eating toxic food and poor levels of health and Fitness. If you actually read everything you probably wouldn't eat any food at all, but I am suggesting that you take an interest. We have to educate ourselves because I for one do not want to be passively contributing to disease in my body just because I don't know, or take an interest in, the dangers of consuming certain foods. Can you substitute one of those meals you eat out for a home-cooked meal? My earlier sentiment about fast food being cheaper is actually more myth than reality (and probably falls more under the convenience spectrum) because you can buy a lot of healthy food at the grocery store if you have a plan when you walk into the store (note: that grocery list we talked about in the Focus chapter is important here). Take some time to assess and log your daily food choices. Can you drink more water during the day instead of always reaching for that soda or sweetened juice? I have lost far too many Family members and friends to diseases such as cancer and diabetes and obesity to just sit back and pretend that I don't see what food is doing to us. Read labels, do your own research, talk to your doctor. There are ways to educate yourself without becoming consumed by all of the negatives associated with food. Take control of this part of Fitness right now and I assure you that you will start seeing immediate benefits in your health and your Family's health. Don't try to do it all at once either, because that approach has failed time and again. Small steps equal big results when it comes to healthy eating as well, just make sure that you don't allow one bad day to become one bad year. While we absolutely cannot control every single thing that we consume, isn't it empowering to think that we have the capability to choose foods that have tangible benefits in our bodies? I for one think that's amazing, and I will continue to exercise that choice at every opportunity.

Football rejection after Football rejection began to take its toll on me and I soon found my life spiraling out of control in late 2007. Guidance for any decision that I made came directly from my lack of Finances and I grew dependent on material admiration rather than my Faith-based foundation and relationships. I alienated many Family members because I was just so unhappy with how things were going and I was completely Focused on the negative circumstances rather than extracting what positive lessons were most definitely present in each. So to illustrate, my Fitness equation looked something like this: (-)Faith + (-)Family + (-)Focus + (-)Finances = (-)Fitness. In our collective Fitness model, all of the individual components were operating at a negative and therefore my Fitness naturally followed that trend. All of that negative energy manifested itself in my body in the form of debilitating migraine headaches. I couldn't concentrate, I couldn't train, I couldn't think of anything but the pain. I tried all sorts of remedies, both through traditional medicine and homeopathic solutions. Nothing worked. I went to the hospital and got a CT-scan on my brain because I actually thought that I was dying. All of the other areas of my life were on life-support and it seems correct that my Fitness and well-being suffered greatly. Well if that wasn't a wake-up call! This is the most life-altering example that I can express to you when it comes to the importance of the individual pieces and their effect on the collective. As I began to slowly repair my Faith, Family, Focus, and Finances, the headaches suddenly stopped. Miracle? Maybe. But I know that it was more than that. It was taking responsibility for my decisions so that I could heal the areas of my life that really needed healing. Only then could I begin to operate at my peak Fitness level.

I want you to expand your thinking of Fitness as more than just a linear equation. Think of it like this: the good life begins and ends with Fitness. Hold on, are we giving this component maybe a little bit too much credit? I don't think so. We can't work on Faith, Family, Focus and Finances without having optimal Fitness. And without Faith, Family, Focus and Finances, we can't and won't have optimal Fitness. These are not all or nothing propositions and there will likely always be a component that needs some work. It is investing the right amount of time and energy into the parts that are sluggish and giving them that kick start necessary to allow you to operate at your Greater Than The Game peak.

"When I first started training Stevie, I was blown away by his strength and athleticism. I couldn't understand why he hadn't achieved success on the field at the highest level. My only conclusion was this: He was greater than the game."

Marco Borges
Celebrity Fitness Expert

CHAPTER 6

FORGIVENESS

*"Freedom from self imprisonment is the
true meaning of forgiveness"*

Anger. Hurt. Disappointment. Frustration. Resentment. Natural human emotions that we have all experienced at one time or another. Does any of one (or all) of these sound too familiar though? Let me immediately confirm a cold hard fact of life for you: we will always be disappointed by people and situations in our lives. Sounds pretty gloomy doesn't it? Well it is reality and we cannot escape it for the simple reason that we cannot control what other people do and say, no matter how hard we may try. All of those things that you would have done under similar circumstances? Don't count on someone else doing the same. As much as you may try to protect yourself from unpleasant feelings, we are all vulnerable to these destructive emotions for the simple fact that we are human; however, each of us is completely different, with differing motivations and values. The sooner that you are able to accept this harsh reality and learn various coping mechanisms when faced with seemingly offensive situations, the better off that you will be. And I can assure you, most of the time that you do find yourself troubled by another's actions, please remember that those actions are a direct outward reflection of the other person. The behavior has absolutely nothing to do with you. If however, you find yourself constantly consumed by these negative emotions, it is very likely that you are placing far too much emphasis on what was said about you or what was done to you.

What if I told you that there is a very simple cure for those feelings. A cure that doesn't include eating a tub of ice cream, or walking around like the entire world owes you something. The cure is quite simple in theory, but exceedingly more difficult in practice because it is by far the most personal concept that I will address in this entire book. The cure is Forgiveness. Contrary to everything that you have probably ever heard, I believe that the ability to Forgive is one of the most selfish acts that we can practice. Sound strange and totally backwards to those early lessons about Forgiveness that you were taught when your little brother or sister stole the toy that you wanted to play with? Possibly, but think about it like this: when you truly are able to Forgive someone, the majority of the benefits flowing from that Forgiveness come directly back to you. So it can be our little secret that Forgiveness is actually a very selfish practice that does not benefit the other party even half as much as it benefits you. I would personally recommend choosing Forgiveness at every opportunity and I challenge you to watch how easily those harmful feelings just melt away.

"I Forgive you." Step one is saying the words. This may be the most difficult part for you. If that is the case for you personally, then I believe that it is your ego driving your inability to Forgive. We all know that one person who just won't accept an apology. For anything. That person who would rather argue a moot point until he or she is blue in the face than to simply say, "it's ok. I forgive you. Let's move on." If you fall into this category, the answer is easy. Start choosing Forgiveness over argument. Stop holding onto pointless grudges against people that you care about just to prove that you are right. Stop it right now! Life is far too short to resent people for human mistakes that we all make. The day that you are perfect is the day that perhaps I will entertain all of the reasons why you cannot Forgive. Until then, Forgive. And start doing it as soon as possible. Never take a precious opportunity to Forgive for granted because as we know, life changes in the blink of an eye. That moment of Forgiveness may never arise again and Forgiveness can take on a whole new and much more difficult meaning under totally different circumstances.

For the majority of us, it is not saying the words "I Forgive you", but meaning and believing in those words. Sure we have all said it. And then left the situation with the same feelings of anger, hatred, disappointment etc. that we started with. So what happens in this case? What happens when we try our very best to Forgive but just can't do it? I know that you won't like this answer, but you keep trying. You keep trying and trying and trying until you actually Forgive the person or situation or place or thing from your inner being. This takes practice. This takes patience and understanding and compassion. This is far from easy! But at the end of the long road, Forgiveness is so worth it because as I previously stated, the self-ish benefits to truly Forgiving are invaluable.

I wouldn't be human if I said that I have never been hurt by people that I care deeply about. From personal relationships, to friendships, to Family feuds – I would like to think that I have done a fairly good job of Forgiving people that I feel may have done me wrong over the years because I know that I have required Forgiveness more times than I care to share. And you know what they say, what goes around comes around, right? It was in the Football context that I was not do-ing such a great job. My high school dream was to attend Florida State University on a full athletic scholarship. In my mind, I had done all that I could with respect to training and showcasing my talent on game day; now all I needed was coach to get on board. I distinctly remember going into his office one afternoon and saying, "hey coach, we need to send my game tape to Florida State." The response that I got was something I would have never imagined coming out of his mouth: "You can't play at Florida State, Stevie. You just can't." I believed that I needed coach to get behind me, to get my name out there, to enlighten recruiters as to my Football and athletic ability. And here he was, telling me that I couldn't do it. For a few years I placed blame directly on coach's shoulders because I convinced myself that he single-handedly ruined my chance to secure an athletic scholarship at the only school I cared anything about. I wholeheartedly believed that he didn't do everything in his power to help me.

I went to Bethune-Cookman that fall with a huge, gigantic chip on my shoul-der. I didn't want to be there, I wanted to be playing Football at Florida State! My attitude towards Football suffered because I held such resentment towards coach that I couldn't Focus on what I needed to do in order to excel at the collegiate level. Herein lies the rub, my personal feelings towards coach didn't affect him at all. I am sure he was going about his daily activities, coaching the Lake Brantley Football team as if nothing happened. But those emotions in my body? They were severely interfering with my mental and physical state. I kept wishing that it had been different, that somehow he would have believed in my ability, that he would have done more. Shortly thereafter, after a particularly difficult game, I made a conscious decision to Forgive coach and to this day it remains the most empowering thing that I have ever done for myself. I didn't have to actually say the words, "I Forgive you", to him, but I had to wholeheartedly believe in them personally. I absolutely had to take away the power that I was giving to those feelings because they would have buried me had I let them. Truthfully, I didn't necessarily know for certain that coach didn't believe in me, I only convinced myself of that part of the story because it fit into my version of events. We so often write a story in our minds that has little or nothing to do with reality. The story is only a reflection of the thoughts and feelings that pervade us and that story is the majority of the time, entirely fictional. Choosing to Forgive coach didn't affect him at all and like I said before, this is how it will play out the majority of the time. You will receive all of the benefits of Forgiving, even if you are the Forgiver. Sometimes Forgiving will prove entirely beneficial to both parties but that actually doesn't matter to me right now. I am interested in Forgiveness' effects on you personally. I care only about you at this exact moment and if I had any doubts as to the value of Forgiving, I would have thought of another concept to write about. If I am completely honest with you, there were so many other ways that I could have been more proactive in securing the scholarship like sending out game tape myself, or enlisting the help of another trusted mentor. I didn't lose an athletic scholarship because of coach, and I knew that it was time to one hundred percent Forgive both him and the situation before the crippling feelings that I internalized and lived daily took away valuable Football opportunities.

It is important to understand the power that not addressing a situation which requires Forgiveness from you may have. You may not consciously think about it, but that terrible in the feeling in the pit of your stomach? That's your body's way of telling you that you are not ok. Forgiveness is a long and sometimes very lonely road. As with any difficult task, taking the required steps to truly Forgive is always worth it. I really can't stress that enough. Forgiveness doesn't necessarily mean that you agree with the situation or that you will let someone walk all over you. It means that you value your personal health and happiness over and above holding a grudge. It means that you refuse to take a version of the story that you don't really know is entirely true, and make it your life. The bitter feelings that infect your body and mind are never worth proving a point. By Forgiving someone, you are giving them one of the greatest gifts available for us to bestow on another human being. And in turn, you are giving yourself an even greater gift.

To that end, there is only one thing more powerful than Forgiving someone, and that is Forgiving yourself. I spent a very long time personally reflecting on all of the negative feelings that I held towards people involved in my Football career over 9 years: the scout that didn't rank me high on his recruiting list; the GM that decided to sign another player; the coach that didn't give me any playing time; the agent that told me that, "no team wants you" and I had better find someone else to represent me. Slowly but surely, I went through all the emotions associated with Forgiveness and I realized that I placed all of the blame on various third parties. In my mind, they were all equally and jointly at fault that I didn't have a long and illustrious career in the NFL or the CFL. Until one day I woke up, went through the same Forgiveness exercise that I did with coach, and in the process realized the single most humbling fact of all time: absolutely not one of those people was actually to blame for anything to do with my Football career. Naturally then, all of that blame that I had so very nicely apportioned out had to fall somewhere, and that somewhere was directly onto my shoulders in the form of debilitating guilt. I didn't work hard enough. I didn't take the appropriate steps to put myself in front of the necessary people. I didn't make the phone calls. I didn't make the on-field plays when I was given the opportunity. And so on it went. I was depressed, I felt alone and I didn't know what to do.

A light bulb went off one day, and I thought, if I have become so proficient at forgiving other people, why can't I forgive myself? I am worthy of Forgiveness too, aren't I? It was like a wave of calm instantly washed over my entire body. I was free. I was Forgiven because I had finally made the decision that I was worth the same treatment that I was affording other people. And it is really that simple. It is making a conscious decision to invest in your happiness in the form of letting go because Forgiving yourself is the most personal and beneficial commitment that you can make to yourself. You don't wear a sign announcing, "I forgave myself", but you will notice that the way you carry yourself changes. The way that you think about yourself changes. You will begin to hold yourself in higher regard. I am here to remind you if it has somehow slipped your mind, that you deserve to be Forgiven by you! For the first time in many years I actually believed that I could continue on my life journey, without Football, in the peace that I know that God wants for all of us. Isn't it amazing that so often we treat other people differently, and often times better, than we treat ourselves? That has to stop immediately. I urge you to Forgive yourself for all of the things you did, and didn't do, and wish you did, and wish you didn't do. The time to let go of all of that negative power is right now. We cannot change the past but we can make immense strides in personal growth by embracing the important lessons that Forgiveness teaches; none of which is more important than the simple fact that we are all flawed, but we are also infinitely worthy of Forgiveness. From other people, and especially from within. God always Forgives, and we must do the same.

When you Forgive, you are essentially releasing all of those negative emotions that you have stored up inside and in turn, you are releasing any power that they hold over you. It is only logical now that you will now have that equal positive power to use for far more beneficial endeavors. Our failures are not what define us, but rather we are defined by how we move through our failures, or those instances where we require Forgiveness of ourselves and others. Some people remain in a perpetual state of failure because it is easier to bathe in guilt, shame and pity than to bask in the light of owning your failures, Forgiving yourself, and Forgiving those who may have wronged you. Only when you Forgive can you move forward in the light of everything that you are called to be. Remember, your demons only stay with you if you let them. When I was able to Forgive myself and all of those people that I mentioned with respect to my Football career, I opened myself up to other incredible career opportunities. I have been so fortunate to explore a passion for movies and television through various acting jobs. A passion that I didn't even know existed inside of me. In turn those acting opportunities have allowed me to continue my philanthropic efforts in a much more meaningful sense. I ultimately allowed myself to be open to these new opportunities because I finally Forgave, released the stranglehold of the negative, and allowed myself to shine without the Football shadow casting any doubt on my self-worth and ability to thrive.

When I say that a whole new world will open up to you right before your very eyes, I am living proof of that fact. I used to think it was Football or bust. I lived for Football and I thought I would die by Football. When it came down to it though, it was only when I finally Forgave Football that I began to live again. Forgiveness in its most pure and true sense lead me to live my Greater Than The Game life every second of every day. Not just part of the day, or yesterday, or maybe tomorrow. So that whole selfish part? Shhhhh … I won't tell if you don't.

"Stevie Baggs is one of the classiest young men that I've ever met. He is wise beyond his years and one tremendously gifted football player..."

Larry Little
NFL Hall of Fame

CHAPTER 7

FOOTBALL

"My greatest teacher"

America's game. Millions of people gather around television screens throughout the world every Sunday, Monday (and now Thursday too), to watch NFL
Football. The billion dollar industry does more than just entertain us. It connects
us. Maybe it's by geography, or by alma mater, or by favorite player. Football
makes us feel as if we all have something in common, at least for the three hours
between kick off and the last second of the fourth quarter. That tie that binds us
is the love of, in my opinion, the greatest game on earth; however, buried deep
within the glitz and glamour of the bright lights and the superhero players wear-
ing your favorite jersey is the ugly side of Football. The side that most of the world
isn't privy to. I often think to myself, if people knew just how ugly Football really
is, would they still love it as much as they do now? And I always come up with
the same answer: yes of course they would. Football broke my heart in a million
pieces. Over, and over, and over again. And to this day I still love it. I love the
excitement and the drama and the competition and the dedication that it takes
to play Football at the highest level. I still love everything that's positive about the
game because I was able to step back and remember it was for all of these positive
reasons that I started playing Football in the first place.

Being a 'Football player' used to define me in everything that I did. I realized
however, that the limitations and power that I was allowing Football to have on
my life when I thought about it this way were holding me back in a major way.
I now choose to say that Football refined me through all of the takeaways that
I embraced throughout my journey. As with any game, if you allow it to define

you, it will consume you and bury you, but if you allow it to refine you, you are all the better equipped to continue on in your life's purpose. I am Greater Than The Game because of the game. Does that make sense? I have translated the set-backs, disappointments and heartbreaks that Football forced upon me and turned those experiences into set-ups for my continuing journey. I appreciate and accept that Football prepared me to recognize the value of the 7 F's, and had it not been for Football, I might be living a mediocre life, none the wiser and certainly unequipped to tell this story. That to me is a much more frightening proposition than following my dreams and becoming frustrated at certain points along the way. My question for you is, will you continue to pursue the game, or will you embrace what the game has taught you so that you can live Greater Than The Game?

I was faced with this very same question in the offseason of the 2008 CFL Football season. Was I prepared to continue to chase the Football dream, risking disappointment all over again? Or was it time to thank Football for everything that it had given me and move on to other goals and aspirations that I held. At the time though, I wasn't able to understand that saying goodbye to Football didn't have to be about giving up, but instead would be about having the strength to let go of something that wasn't serving me in my growth as a person any longer. It was almost as if I was clenching Football in my fist so tight that nothing else could penetrate my hand. At the time, I looked at giving up as a straight failure of my lifelong dream.

If you knew me at this point in my life, you would know that my appearance was quite different than it is today because I wore my hair in dreadlocks. In fact, I had not had a haircut in over 4 years since my time at Bethune-Cookman. My hair defined me, the same way that I felt Football defined me. So when I told my mother and stepfather that I was considering cutting my hair, they knew that what I really meant was that I was considering giving up on Football altogether.

I eventually took jobs with my mentor and close friend, Demaral, helping him with his transportation business, and as a substitute teacher. As for the haircut, I held off for the time being. I still wasn't too sure about Football although I continued training, just in case. But instead of worrying about that next opportunity and that next contract, or defining my life by the lack of opportunity or contract, I lived in the Faith that if it was meant to be, it would happen. Of course miraculously mid-season I got my best contract offer and I went on to play two and a half great years of Football. And you know why I finally tasted that elusive success after all of those failed attempts at Football? I put into practice all of the things that we have touched upon in the preceding chapters. Just in case you had any doubt as to the value of that cheat sheet I mentioned at the beginning of the book, I can assure you that the concepts are 100% are tried, tested and true. In 2009, I wrote down my goals just like in college: 1) start every game; 2) stay healthy for the entire season and post-season; 3) lead the CFL in sacks; 4) earn a spot on the CFL all-start team; 5) earn defensive player of the year. I didn't quite make it with respect to the last goal, but I came very close and that is enough for me today. I had a great relationship with my teammates and with the community in Regina, Saskatchewan, I was in the best shape of my life, and I didn't go to sleep at night worrying about how I was going to pay my bills. I was operating at the pinnacle of my game because I had all of the tools of Faith, Family, Focus, Finances, Fitness and Forgiveness working together to ensure that I would be successful. I was living Greater Than The Game.

When I finally cut my hair, it had nothing to do with the fact that I was done playing Football, but everything to do with honoring the gifts that Football has given me. I opened up my fingers and released the power that Football held over my life. I was finally open to receive all of the things that had been waiting for me while I was holding on too tight. At the same time, I channeled Football's power towards me, this time in a positive direction. Football will eat you up, spit you out, and then try to do it all over again when it thinks that you've forgotten about it. The same goes for life. I refused to be defined by those disappointments and used my last release from the Hamilton Tiger Cats in 2011 not as another heartbreak, but as an opportunity to re-launch and redefine my line of thinking. I was greater than Football for the simple fact that I had finally accepted its purpose in my life.

Aside from the 7 F's, Football has taught me so much more about Stevie Baggs Jr. as a human being. Playing on different teams all over the world, living in subpar conditions or with teammates in cramped motels, I learned to be versatile. Being told that I would never play professionally because of the way that I walk, I learned perseverance and the value of a strong work ethic. Always being on the verge of making a team, but never quite securing a position on the roster taught me to be optimistic, that there was always another chance waiting around the corner. Tasting success but still appreciating the long and difficult journey that got me there reminds me to always stay humble, no matter how good life may seem at a particular moment. I believe that my Football journey is the equivalent of any other life journey. A journey that each one of you has taken to get you to exactly where you are standing right now. Because of that, I can empathize with each of you as I am confident that you have had an equally demanding climb to the present moment. But here we are, standing tall, standing proud, standing in the light of everything that we are called to be.

Throughout my career I have been chastised for having celebrations after a play that some consider too excessive. People didn't hesitate to label me as arrogant or showy. For me, the celebration after a play simply allowed me to express what I had been through, and reminded me why I continued to play Football. The celebration also gave me hope for the next play. Remember this the next time someone says that you are 'showing off'. If you don't celebrate yourself, who will? Celebrate yourself to motivate, honor and respect all of the things that your game has given to you and all of the things that you have overcome to allow you to stand alongside me right now. Maybe you lost ten pounds after sticking with a new Fitness regime. Celebrate that. Maybe you enrolled in an evening course to study a new skill. Celebrate that. I am here to join in your celebration and remind you that you are amazing simply because you are here. If this is the only thing that you take from the book, I will still consider it a success. Once again if you didn't catch it the first time, you are amazing. You have one chance at making your life everything that it is meant to be. Own it. Live it. Love it.

Given that we are nearing the end of our journey together, it is time to connect the dots. Thinking back to our discussion about each of the 7 F's, we can see that there is one constant throughout those chapters and if you recognize that recurring theme to be power, you get an A+ on the final exam. Coupled with that power is choice. It is time to consciously choose to release the power that each of the applicable F's has on our lives and use it to our advantage. Power doesn't do any good if you are not prepared to take the steps to release the power and use the advantages of that power in your life on a daily basis. Faith taps into the power of the unknown, the spiritual, the supernatural, the power of relationships and love. Family draws on the power of relationships, being held to a higher standard and motivation. With Focus we see the power of organization, intention, and mindfulness at work, while Finances remind us to be inspired of the power of a greater purpose has. Fitness channels the incredible power of the human body and its desire to be our living breathing vessel for greatness. Forgiveness finally relies on the power of letting go. The power of Football might be more applicable to my life, but whatever your game is, there is particular power to be drawn from the experience, no matter how dark that it might seem on the surface. Each of the 7 F's is a piece of the shield of armor that you wear when you continue to move forward on the journey of life. Translating the power that the game, or external concept that you identify with, holds over you in a negative way, and redirecting the energy back to yourself with positive intention is the key to living your best life. Living free in your Greater Than The Game life is nothing more than recognizing that your self-worth is not tied to the external game circumstance, disappointment, failure or experience, and utilizing the power to understand your worth far beyond the confines of the game. No matter what happens, no matter what adversity or upbringing or career or situation is holding you back, you are greater than all of it for the simple fact that you have the power to be greater. And now you have the important choice to decide whether you will utilize the tools to channel that power to be greater.

In college my teammates gave me the nickname "Shakespeare" because all I did was make plays. The name stuck with throughout my Football career and in my darkest days, I believed that the nickname was a curse. Most of Shakespeare's plays were tragedies, I thought to myself, so was my story going to turn out exactly the same? Another miserable ending? No. My story didn't turn out the same because I didn't let it turn out the same. I had the power to say that this isn't good enough, I will do better. You too have the pen and paper which has composed your story thus far, and now you have the added power of the 7 F's to lead your writing in a new direction. Use your game as the motivation to keep writing, to create a new path if required, and to confirm for yourself that you are destined to write a best-seller. I look forward to reading your personal tale of greatness.

"To be successful in this world requires possessing the 3H's. Stevie definitely posses them. He is hungry, humble, and honest. I've witness his transformation into the man he is today because of these attributes."

Milt Stegall
CFL Hall of Fame

CHAPTER 8

FUTURE

"Fundamentals, Understanding, Truth,
Unity, Reality, Empowerment"

"He rested on the 7th day from all his work..." The biblical story of creation reminds us that in the spiritual realm, the number 7 is associated with completion. It is for this very reason that I chose to reflect on the 7 F's; however, I believe that our journey is ongoing and once we have completed one cycle of growth and transformation, we are meant to begin another. With that, I am reminded that the number 8 is connected to rebirth, new meaning and fresh beginnings. What better way to celebrate the awareness that we are all Greater Than The Game than to develop a strategy as to how we will utilize all of the tools going forward. The most exciting part of our journey together in my opinion, is that we are moving forward in an enhanced state of mind, not allowing the mistakes of the past block the present moment. So let's head into the 8th F, the Future...

It is impossible to move forward without laying the groundwork for living the Greater Than The Game life. It is here that we must appreciate that the fundamentals behind of each of the principles are the most important. If you do not have a handle on the concepts at the most basic level, it is difficult to utilize the principle to elevate your game in practice. The fundamentals lie within our ability to find the key to unlocking the power and value of each of the 7 F's. At this crucial first level we are the students of the principles, soaking in the significance and usefulness of each and honoring the personal value as applicable to our lives. What works for me, may not exactly work for you so it is about recognizing that difference and manipulating the concepts to create the basis of your Greater Than The Game lifestyle.

Once we have a handle on the fundamentals, we are called to truly understand the gifts of the past, how fortunate we are to be living in the present, and most importantly the purpose of the Future. Many think that the Future is a mystery, but I do not look at it this way. The Future only remains a mystery when you have no vision or understanding of your true purpose. Through the 7 F's I encourage you to embark on that journey of understanding what you have been called to do. Write, reflect, share, encourage yourself, really think about what passions motivate you to live your best life. It is through this understanding of yourself that the world opens its doors to you.

What do you see when you look at the person staring back in the mirror? Are you masking the pain and hurt that lives deep within you by forcing a smile? Trust me, we can all see through that. Whatever feelings are living on your heart, those emotions manifest themselves to your physical being. You can only hide behind expensive clothes and pretty makeup for so long before the ugliness of a damaged interior will be exposed. Living in the truth of all of your experiences, good and bad, will allow the beauty of the healing process to glow. The scars might still be there, but they will continue to fade and will eventually serve only as gentle reminders of how far you have travelled. Your Future burns brightest when you recognize and accept that your truth is the only one worth living.

You have accepted the power and value of the 7 F's at work in your life, but in order to put them into practice you must move beyond the abstract. Unifying the concepts to work as one collective model ultimately allows the conceptual to operate appropriately in reality. Unity is what brings it all together for us. How do we accomplish that seamless transition? Work within the context of your life. All of the people, places, experiences that are personal to you will form the operational framework for the 7 F's. Because none of us will be able to draw upon identical life experiences, the unification process is quite unique. There is no right or wrong answer as to how to put it all together for yourself because every perspective is different. I know that I have read philosophical work that I just can't wrap my head, and not because it doesn't have value, but because I can't quite figure out how it applies to my life. The straightforward nature of the concepts at their basic level allows us to unify and apply them to our Future without the need for impossibly-complex analysis.

Moving past the theoretical, I don't want you to think that putting the 7 F's into practice will be a daunting task, requiring endless time that you probably don't have. I want you to open yourself up and let reality be your guide. I've said it before and I will say it again, if it can't be applied to your specific situation, change it! My stories and resulting analysis are meant to guide the situations that shape your Future in real time. I want you to take Greater Than The Game as more than words on a page and commit to yourself that you will practically apply the principles in your personal reality. I said earlier that if you don't remember one specific thing that happened to me, that was ok. I think that is much more than ok because if you are able to live the 7 F's according to your reality, you are actually setting up the most important Future that there is, your own.

I am going to leave you with something that may not make a lot of sense at first glance, but something that I believe to the very core of my being. Beyond the job, career, lifestyle, gender, race, socioeconomic status, I believe that each of us living today has the same ultimate purpose in life. Sound backward to everything that I have said so far? Maybe on the surface but think deeper. Think beyond yourself. I believe that our most important purpose is to empower others to live their own Greater Than The Game lifes. I believe that we are called to live this collective purpose through the unique gifts that we have cultivated along our own personal journey of life. If you truly understand Greater Than The Game then you will understand that not only do we become greater individually through the journey, we are required to empower others in becoming greater as well. Whether or not we are able to rise up to this ultimate purpose is a totally different story. I challenge you to accept your supreme calling to become Greater Than The Game by empowering others to use the past to live in the glory of the present with the promise of an amazing F.U.T.U.R.E.

"There is a difference
between being on a paper
chase and a purpose chase"

Stevie "Shakespeare" Baggs Jr.

Clockwise from left: Stevie Baggs Jr.(#52 Bethune-Cookman University 2003); Rosa Cannon (Grandmother 2011); Stevie Baggs Jr. (#21 Lake Brantley High School Retired Jersey 2010)

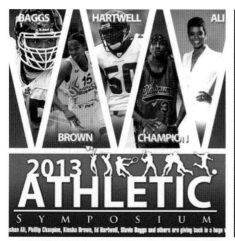

BAGGS HARTWELL ALI

BROWN CHAMPION

2013 ATHLETIC

S Y M P O S I U M

...shan Ali, Phillip Champion, Kiesha Brown, Ed Hartwell, Stevie Baggs and others are giving back in a huge w...

STEVIE:
Professional Football Player, Actor, Model and Catalyst Fitness Client

Clockwise from upper left: Stevie at Tyler Perry Studios 2013 as officer Baker (For Better or Worse); Stevie Speaking at a CETA Foundation HIV/AIDS awareness event 2009; Will Smith, Lola Cannon-Robinson (Mother), Stevie at an NFL sons and mothers event 2004; Stevie speaking to students at B.E.S.T. Academy school in Atlanta 2013.

Clockwise from upper left: Devin Baggs (brother), Stevie Baggs Sr (Father), Stevie Jr. 2012;
Bernice Baggs (Grandmother), Stevie/Lola Cannon-Robinson (Mother), Stevie;
Lola, Raje Robinson (sister)/Rosa Cannon (Grandmother), Francis Cannon (Aunt),
Makiya Mack (sister), Perry Robinson (Step-Father), Malik Robinson (brother), Stevie 2008

Clockwise from upper left: Calgary Stampeders/Baltimore Ravens 2012; Ray Lewis and Stevie 2008; Stevie and Mike Tomlin 2009; Stevie and Deacon Jones 2010; Stevie Baggs Saskatchewan Roughriders 2009; Stevie Baggs Arizona Cardinals 2010.

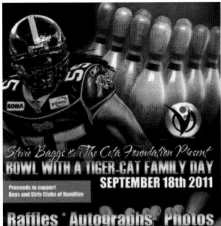

Stevie Baggs Jr.

Stevie Baggs Jr. is a three-time All-American and graduate of Bethune Cookman University. Many know him for his athletic career in the NFL and CFL. Recognized as the only athlete to play for 11 professional football teams, Baggs accounts how his experience prepared him for a purpose beyond the stadium with his soon-to-be released book, titled *Greater Than the Game*. Since his 10 years in football, Baggs has been empowering the youth and adults nationwide with motivational speaking, honored as the City of Atlanta's Health & Wellness Ambassador by Mayor Kasim Reed, and recently celebrated the CETA Foundation's 11th year of service to risk communities. If you have never witnessed him on the field or in your community, you may have spotted him on television shows like Tyler Perry's, *For Better or Worse* (Season 3), or the USA network's, *Necessary Roughness*. Next, be on the look out for Baggs on the big screen in *Focus* with Will Smith, coming spring 2015.

Motivational Speaking

Baggs is considered widely as one of Atlanta's top rising stars of today and future leaders of tomorrow. Often called to deliver messages of inspiration, Baggs uses his professional sport career as leverage to impact a diverse audiences across the world. Through his humble attitude and gracious service to the community, Baggs has garnered the support and partnership of many renown charitable, educational, health and sports organizations such as the following:

• The Boys & Girls Club

• The 100% Wrong Club, FCA (Fellowship of Christian Athletes)

• Students In Free Enterprise (SIFE)